Typography and Motion Graphics

In his latest book, Michael Betancourt explores the nature and role of typography in motion graphics as a way to consider its distinction from static design using the concept of the 'reading-image' to model the ways that motion typography dramatizes the process of reading and audience recognition of language on-screen. Using both classic and contemporary title sequences—including *The Man With the Golden Arm* (1955), *Alien* (1979), *Flubber* (1998), *Six Feet Under* (2001), *The Number 23* (2007), and *Scott Pilgrim vs. The World* (2010)—Betancourt develops an argument about what distinguishes motion graphics from graphic design. Moving beyond title sequences, Betancourt also analyzes moving or kinetic typography in logo designs, commercials, film trailers, and information graphics, offering a striking theoretical model for understanding typography in media.

Michael Betancourt is a research artist/theorist concerned with digital technology and capitalist ideology. His writing has been translated into Chinese, French, German, Greek, Italian, Persian, Portuguese, and Spanish, and published in journals such as *The Atlantic*, *Make Magazine*, *CTheory*, and *Leonardo*. He is the author of *The ___________ Manifesto*, and books such as *The History of Motion Graphics*, and *The Critique of Digital Capitalism*, as well as three books on the semiotics of motion graphics: *Semiotics and Title Sequences*, *Synchronization and Title Sequences*, and *Title Sequences as Paratexts*. These publications complement his movies, which have screened internationally at the Black Maria Film Festival, Art Basel Miami Beach, Contemporary Art Ruhr, Athens Video Art Festival, Festival des Cinemas Differents de Paris, Anthology Film Archives, Millennium Film Workshop, the San Francisco Cinematheque's Crossroads, and Experiments in Cinema, among many others.

Routledge Studies in Media Theory & Practice

1 **Semiotics and Title Sequences**
Text-Image Composites in Motion Graphics
Authored by Michael Betancourt

2 **Synchronization and Title Sequences**
Audio-Visual Semiosis in Motion Graphics
Authored by Michael Betancourt

3 **Title Sequences as Paratexts**
Narrative Anticipation and Recapitulation
Authored by Michael Betancourt

4 **The Screenwriters Taxonomy**
A Collaborative Approach to Creative Storytelling
Authored by Eric R. Williams

5 **Open Space New Media Documentary**
A Toolkit for Theory and Practice
Patricia R. Zimmermann and Helen De Michiel

6 **Film & TV Tax Incentives in the U.S.**
Courting Hollywood
Authored by Glenda Cantrell and Daniel Wheatcroft

7 **Typography and Motion Graphics**
The 'Reading-Image'
Authored by Michael Betancourt

Typography and Motion Graphics

The 'Reading-Image'

Michael Betancourt

Routledge
Taylor & Francis Group
LONDON AND NEW YORK

First published 2019 by Routledge
2 Park Square, Milton Park, Abingdon, Oxon OX14 4RN
52 Vanderbilt Avenue, New York, NY 10017

Routledge is an imprint of the Taylor & Francis Group, an informa business

Library of Congress Cataloging in Publication Data
A catalog record has been requested for this book

ISBN: 978-0-367-02928-9 (hbk)

Typeset in Times New Roman
by Out of House Publishing

For Leah

Contents

Figures

Acknowledgments

The 'reading-image' emerged from many disparate conversations over several years, and would not have been possible without the discussions and assistance from many people who contributed observations, suggested references or works, and discussed the ideation. The aid of my colleagues Dominique Elliott, John Colette, James Gladman, Austin Shaw, Minho Shin, and Woon ("Duff") Yong; as well as my graduate students Jordan Adams, Noël Anderson, Moira ("MoMo") Burke, Joel Desmond, Dominica Jordan, Muge Mahmutcavusoglu, Amanda Quist, Eryn Reiple, and Matt Van Rys has proven essential to its development. Special thanks go to my brother, John Betancourt, for his assistance with locating many of the title sequences that inform this study, and to Louise Sandhaus for her help with the commercials.

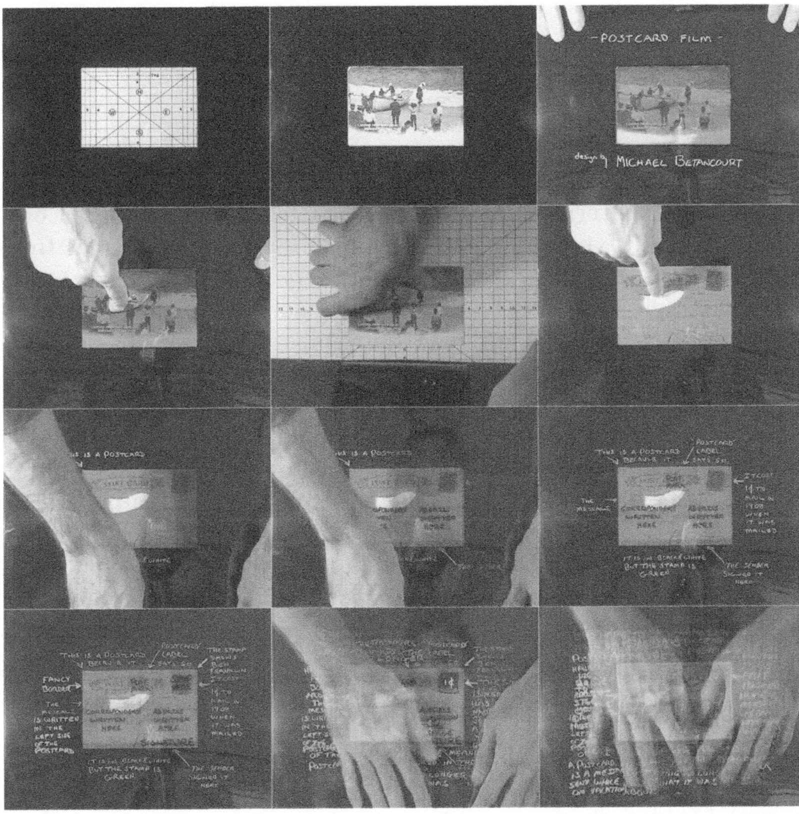

Frontis Stills from *Postcard Film* © 1999 Michael Betancourt / Artists Rights Society (ARS). This movie creates a 'reading-image' (*chronic progression*) using a combination of imaging technologies superimposed as a palimpsest: photolithographic postcard of a beach scene in New Jersey from 1896, 16 mm film shot on an animation stand, digital video, and finally the electronic compositing possibilities of the digital computer to compress and expand time while merging footage from various sources

Motion Typography

Formal aesthetic criteria provide only a partial understanding of how movement and typography interact; the present study emerges from the question, "*How is typography in motion graphics different from graphic design?*" Reflecting on this ontological question leads to a consideration of the role that *kinesis* (movement on-screen) has for typography and graphic elements as a corollary to their lexical structure. Animated typography creates a profusion of new meanings linked to its semiosis, which the 'reading-image' identifies as a dramatization of the recognition process being visualized on-screen (what has been described as an affect[1] of *Schriftfilme* [*textfilm*][2]—motion pictures in which text becomes image-in-motion). This excess to lexical meaning complements the familiar role of written language: movement is an enunciative action the audience interprets fluently based on their past experiences with static and motion typography, and which reflects their established lexical and interpretive proficiency with rendering visual perceptions into the categories of graphics, imagery, and typography.

Specific to motion graphics, if not a necessary and sufficient condition of its definition, *motion typography* is a prominent and common feature.[3] Although the formal morphology and structure of static design appears in the various uses and applications of on-screen typo/graphics, this convergence is a symptom of the challenges it offers for static design. Motion graphics are *not* just graphic design plus animation.[4] Instead, motion graphics are primarily concerned with the new semiosis that structured time offers to design, arrangement, and presentation on-screen. The differences that actual, literal time and motion make for design are, ultimately, conclusive.

Contemporary digital animation software generates a broad spectrum of animations for typography, including the shape-changing of individual letterforms in animorphs, as well as the visual effects (VFX) compositing of typography within live action footage.[5] Books on the production techniques for motion typography reveal a consistent approach to the dynamics offered by animation. The aesthetics and traditions established by earlier technologies remain apparent in the self-similarity of all motion typography, whatever their mode of production: as the technical restraints on animated typography have gradually vanished with the invention of newer, more precise, and cost-effective technologies, the same processes and interpretive engagements remain, despite the changes. The 'reading-image' emerges from this history in three variations that are defined by different, discrete roles for *kinesis*—time and movement within the visual composition of the screen. Understanding motion typography through this set of closely knit theoretical dimensions reveals *kinetic action*, *graphic expression*, and *chronic progression* as distinct modes linked to specific engagements with on-screen motion.

Although motion typography appears in advertising films, TV commercials, interactive software, web page designs and the brief logo animations, "bumpers" or idents used in broadcasting (in addition to title sequences), all these examples of animated typography are not uniformly available for critical consideration. The proliferation of kinetic media—computer screens, televisions, billboards, and even e-books—testifies to the vastly lowered production costs for historically expensive, highly complex, and labor-intensive animation processes; however, even the most expensive animations and compositing are typically ephemeral, neither designed to be memorable nor much remembered. Unlike other kinds of motion picture, such as feature films, motion graphics tend to disappear as quickly as their topicality and novelty fade: this aspect of motion typography complicates simple research activities—i.e. *collection*—beyond its familiar appearance in title sequences. Since there are far more instances of motion typography in use than appear in title designs, the examples in this analysis were drawn from a wide range of sources in video art, experimental film, and commercial title sequences—not because of any particular priority, but because the works discussed have remained readily accessible over time. This issue of access coupled with their role as exemplars of "type" justifies the selections based on their utility for identifying the principles under consideration. Special consideration was given to designs made *before* digital animation technology was available, thus revealing the independence of the 'reading-image' from digital processing and technology. Carefully curating this limited, archival approach gives the resulting analysis a breadth beyond simply a consideration of the "hot" designs of the contemporary moment; thus, the selection reflects the capacity of each example to demonstrate the historical scope developed from a much broader analysis of the 'reading-image' than what is presented herein. This discussion is summative. These selections illustrate how motion graphics in the United States developed in the network of

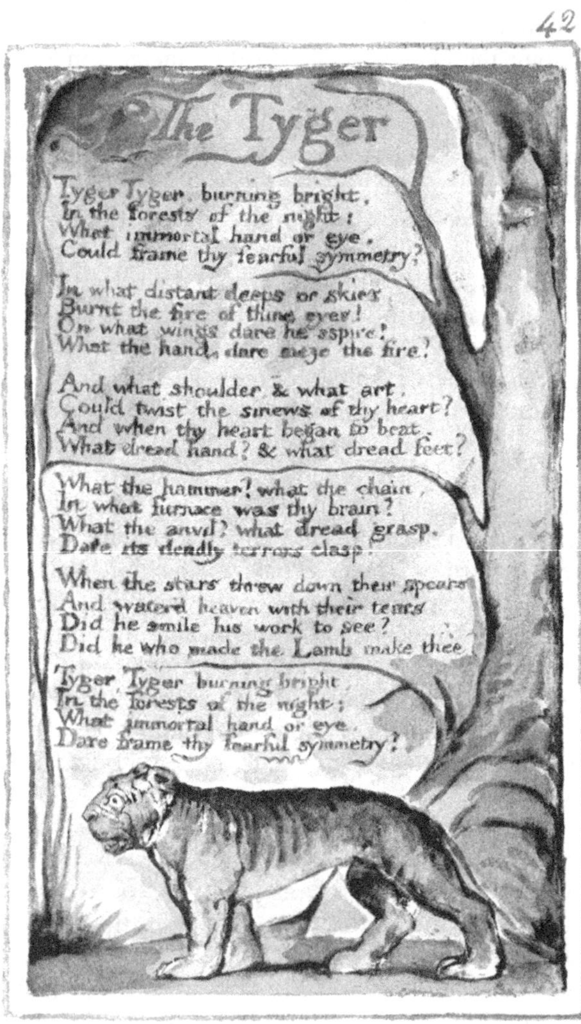

Figure 0.1 "The Tyger" from *Songs of Experience* by William Blake (1794)

connections between Modernism, motion typography, and the historical abstract film as they became commercial, on-screen design.

Beyond mere accessibility, one of the fundamental conceptual barriers to approaching motion typography is its prosaic nature and banality, as graphic designer and theorist Johanna Drucker noted in "What is a Word's Body?" Because print and publishing are not considered "Art" by art history, these products of industrial manufacture have a long history of rejection by and within the art world, with graphic design and typography figuring prominently in that ellipsis of critico-theoretical inattention. Being rejected as kitsch makes considerations of static and motion typography rare in the critical theories of semiotics and philosophy:

> In the twentieth century, mainstream philosophy famously takes what is referred to as "the linguistic turn" [...] but shockingly, totally absent from those accounts is any attention to the visual or material properties of language. No matter where one looks in the texts of Frege, Carnap, Wittgenstein, or Saussure, the materiality, and in particular the visual quality of written language goes unmentioned.[6]

In this essay on the form of *words* in *writing*, Drucker observes that typography is an omission, largely absent from semiotics and art history. The approach in graphic design tends towards a formalist taxonomy, creating a misperception of theoretical engagement by confusing the extensive heuristics ('design theory') *for* type arrangement ('design theory') with theories about or *of* arrangement.[7] In semiotic theory, text and typography is commonly assumed as a 'given,' accepted and discussed without a careful consideration of its own, peculiar dynamics. Semiotician Roman Jakobson is typical. He has written about poetic language and the problems of its interpretation, and provides extensive formal considerations of poet-painters such as William Blake [Figure 0.1]. But in all his careful and detailed analysis, he does not address their visuality—the imagistic dimensions of the compositions, the placement of the text in correspondence to the picture, or the material form of the hand-lettering (failing to even note that it *is* hand-lettering).[8] Considering the lineage of design in European visual culture presents conceptual problems for art history, precisely ignoring the "visual or material properties of language." These refusals of visuality in the semiotics of language and text, like the denial of typography as a domain for consideration, are endemic to serious philosophical and art historical analysis that would otherwise support and might[9] already have proposed the 'reading-image.'

Typography is under-theorized. The great irony of the critical hermeneutics presented by cinema semiotics, such as the work of Christian

Metz, is this same lack of consideration for text-on-screen,[10] with no significant engagement with typography or the specifics of its use in motion pictures. His study *Impersonal Enunciation, or the Place of Film* only addresses text-on-screen in terms of its *narrative function*, as "Written Modes of Address": text is either a relay of dialogue, what he terms "diagetical," or is more specifically expository, what he calls "explanatory titles"[11] that offer specific methods to address the viewers such as subtitles or intertitles (i.e. a title card stating "Meanwhile"). They act as narration for and within a narrative construct, but the formal and visual dimensions of the typography never make an appearance in this analysis. Metz is typical in understanding cinema only in terms of its *narrative function*: this approach is a common feature of its historical explication. Terry Ramsaye's early history of film, *A Million and One Nights* (1924), offered a specific conception tied explicitly to narrative forms.[12] This framework implicitly continued in the French historical account by Maurice Bardèche and Robert Brasillach, *The History of Motion Pictures* (1938),[13] and American author Lewis Jacobs's two editions of *The Rise of the American Film* (1939/1948) serve to demonstrate and affirm the consistency of this equation, *cinema=narrative*,[14] that makes considerations of typography rare and unusual for film history and cinema semiotics.

The 'reading-image' is tangential to these narrative and narrational concerns. Instead of being oriented towards the fictive presentations on-screen, it concerns the interpretive play and engagement of lexicality that is modeled in the animation-presentation itself. Metz's concerns, which align textuality with its metaphoric role as a descriptor for imagery as is typical for considerations of text in cinema, only engage the interpretive effects of narrative.[15] The 'reading-image' describes a translation of thought processes into the presentational dynamics of animation, but with only a few exceptional designs (most apparent in the title sequences of commercial cinema that function as peritexts—those designs linked to and simultaneously independent of the narrative) motion graphics containing animated type are not generally retained or critically appraised, masking this development from historical identification. Considerations of typography in these terms constitute a lacuna in cinema semiotics, revealing the typical equation *cinema=narrative* that justifies ignoring how both avant-garde media and motion graphics employ typography. The 'reading-image' has been ignored primarily because motion typography has not received appropriate critical attention. Metz only notes the role of *design* for the signification of text-on-screen in passing:

> We should also take into account how some titles play with typography, font size, the arrangement of words inside the frame, and so on. These unexpected variations both reinforce and modulate the

> effect of the address insofar as they pointedly attract the gaze and present themselves as enunciative intrusions.[16]

His analysis folds these dynamics into his already established narrative concerns as accentuations; the "enunciative intrusion" conceives the text as only an interruption of the narrative progression, a violation of the diegetic space on-screen. There is no consideration of *how* these dynamics might work beyond *narrative function*, neither what their organization might resemble, nor the distinctions between static and motion type—which he does not address or even mention. Design as a specific enunciation in itself offers an excess to the familiar lexical approaches of written and spoken language, functioning as a contributing element in the presentation of the text, but without the predetermined index of established meanings that enables language to function.[17] Its neglect is logical given the understanding of *cinema=narrative* which places typography outside the realm of consideration, even if it comprises a major absence in existing semiotic theory for motion pictures.

A History of Formalist Approaches

Typography is of great concern to graphic design, which has extensively discussed and considered formal issues of arrangement such as size, leading, or tracking/kerning that inform the higher-level, yet still formal, concerns of legibility and the impacts of layout and placement on the static page. Technical issues of typesetting that inform the visual hierarchy in design are not the same as theoretical and critical appraisals leading to general principles. The most common approach to these formal questions of placement and the capacity of text to support lexical engagement is precisely the Modernist heritage that leads historical graphic design to invisibly prioritize formalist concerns, a dimension more readily and easily grasped and addressed in 'design theory' than the abstract and philosophical dimensions which inform semiosis, leading to a confusion of formal protocols with semiotic theory. This formalist bias defines the parameters of design theory for typography; the graphic designers themselves resist theorizing typography, reflecting this confusion of heuristic and hermeneutic theory.[18] Their refusal demonstrates what semiotician Umberto Eco identified in *A Theory of Semiotics* as indicative of "*text-oriented* culture" (a procedure reified in formalist approaches to design) that employs specific 'models' to emulate, rather than developing a general set of theoretical protocols:

> There are cultures governed by a *system* of rules and there are cultures governed by a *repertoire* of texts imposing models of behavior. In the former category texts are generated by

> combinations of discrete units and are judged correct or incorrect according to their conformity to the combinational rules; in the latter category society directly generates texts, these constituting macro-units from which rules could eventually be inferred, but that first and foremost propose models to be followed and imitated.[19]

The distinction or difference between *grammar-oriented* and *text-oriented* cultures Eco describes is recognizable in the role of 'model texts' for design. This same lack of theoretical discussion about typography also applies to Eco's work, which *en passant* leaves the role of design and typography to be a part of his theory only by extending its implications beyond the organization and structure of semiotic protocols he proposes. In neither proposing nor including issues of typography in his analysis, Eco leaves these dimensions of his theorization as nebulous zones of implied order, but without discrete explanation. It leaves the questions of typography to the specification of models to emulate—what Eco terms a "*text-oriented* culture." The disengagement with theory in graphic design is a reflection of a refusal of general, theoretical principles. Seeking to apply theory instead of engaging its analytic leaves only formalist frameworks to determine the range of allowable outcomes. In place of an identification of combinatory rules, the "repertoire of texts" collected and presented act as a descriptive collection of elements, but without a corresponding set of generative guides that articulate the reasons for that selection. This approach appears in film design theorist Peter von Arx's study *Film Design* (published in 1983).[20] His analysis established a critical engagement with the visuality of motion compositions via a taxonomy of visual forms and structures that links static and motion typography but retains a specifically formalist approach, cataloging perceptual dynamics without a hermeneutic critical framework—a taxonomy of material arrangements of text and type on-screen in relation to graphics and photography. The impacts of the avant-garde 'structural film' are apparent throughout von Arx's project connecting visual music, later avant-garde films, and commercial design. This cinematic heritage is a self-evident element of motion graphics, but is commonly downplayed or even ignored in the consideration of motion typography in studies of static typography that also address movement.

The formal identification of exemplary designs is common in graphic design, apparent in the various books edited by György Kepes during the 1950s and 1960s that catalog important developments and visual examples. The lack of general theorization in an anthology might not be surprising, but it is also absent in his own text *Language of Vision* (published in 1959). The descriptive approach common to all his books matches that of von Arx: it entails a listing of elements and components drawn from models. His anthologies consider then-current and popular topics in design, but without ever addressing either static or motion typography; this absence of analysis is especially evident in *Sign Image Symbol* (published in 1966). Failure to recognize 'motion graphics' as it emerged is a significant omission in these studies. The collection and presentation of exemplars that then become models for other designers is an explicit result of these books' influence. They do not propose general principles for design, instead focusing on the role of cultural signifiers as features that improve the quality of the designs shown; there is no consideration of what the particular rules or guidelines are for these works, instead presenting them as *sui generis* iterations of quality work.

In contrast to the topicality of Kepes, the discussion of typography by Robin Kinross in *Modern Typography* is historical. The analysis of technological and aesthetic innovations from Gutenberg's press to the present day describes the evolution of typography, but does not address the role of motion as a transformation of this historically-conceived description of typographic systems. In tracing the progressive and evolutional lineage, Kinross enables an understanding of the present as the outcome of established and immobile processes that denaturalize history, but at the same time render its 'progress' as a specifically formal derivation of technological innovations.

Other books, such as *Typographic Design: Form and Communication* by Rob Carter, Sandra Maxa, Mark Sanders, Phillip B. Meggs, and Ben Day (first published in 1986 and periodically updated, with the seventh edition published in 2018), offer similar case studies of work by leading designers and design companies, but *not* theories of their visual ordering that link their animation with cinematic concerns, instead approaching them through the framework of static design. The limitations of historical graphic design emerge through its lapses in engagement with motion picture media. This same restricted approach informs *Moving Type: Designing for Time and Space* by Matt Woolman and Jeff Bellantoni (published in 2000), which presents a similar formal system to move letterforms and typography, but is not concerned with theory beyond that needed for the immanent heuristic being presented:

> Moving type is more often than not most successful when presented in individual word or phrase sequences because computer and television screens are an inferior medium for reading long and involved text. Just as we have certain expectations from a book—permanence, a contemplative text on which one can review and meditate—animated typographic sequences are best presented in the form of short sentences or phrases designed to ask a question, simply point in a direction, or provide visual "sound" bites.[21]

The approach Woolman and Bellantoni develop is precisely appropriate for the animated logos and graphics of broadcast design, with its emphasis on attention-catching visuals. Their instructional text does not pause to consider the principles that underlie the approach—such considerations are explicitly beyond the scope of their analysis. These limitations are common for considerations of motion typography, a distinction that separates heuristics from the analytic and considered engagements of hermeneutic, critical theory.

It is normal for studies of typography and design, such as Ellen Lupton and Abbott Miller's *Design Writing Research: Writing on Graphic Design*, to ignore the significance of *movement*, instead considering typography as a consistent material whose morphology and structure are stable.[22] The formalist approach to typography is common to graphic design generally, which avoids the consideration of semiotics (whether Piercian, Saussurean, or those of Eco and the post-structuralists), offering instead a collection of model texts to emulate. The proposition of 'reading-image' accounts for interpretive dynamics absent from formal descriptions; Lupton and Miller's analysis is typical of this absence. There are only a limited number of studies that attempt a theoretical description of morphology and structure for *kinesis*. Christian Leborg's book *Visual Grammar* (published in 2006) is notable because it includes a consideration of *motion* in the section titled "Activities," considering movement not simply as an implied metaphor, but in terms specific to its literal use in motion pictures:

> **Movement.** True movement (without sequences or steps) is only found in the real world. Movement within a visual composition is only a representation of movement. The positioning of an object can suggest forces that have influenced it or will influence it and move it.
>
> **Path.** An object in constant movement will travel along an imagined line. The line is called a path. The path can be straight or have the form of an arc.
>
> **Direction.** The direction of a movement can be defined by a line that leads from the starting point of the movement to its presumed end point.
>
> **Superordinate and Subordinate Movement.** An object can rotate, swing, or move forward and backward, while still experiencing a superordinate movement along one path.[23]

His highly reductive description is accompanied by elaborate illustrations that inform his discussion, making their relevance for motion pictures explicit. The identification of elements through formalist analyses separates the meaning of model texts and taxonomic classifications from how this descriptive system creates meaning. The diagrammatic approach employed by Leborg renders his schematic proposal as a series of graphics whose minimal design ensures their clarity of presentation. The formalist dimensions of this proposal are an implicit feature of its execution; the conception of motion—including in motion typography—becomes for his proposal simply one more element within the lexicon of graphic design, a subsumption of motion graphics to this familiar, established field.

Motion typography poses a significant lacuna in the theoretical analysis of typography. The historical survey *Typemotion*, edited by Bernd Scheffer, Christine Stenzer, Peter Weibel, and Soenke Zehle (published in 2015), notes that the lengthy history of motion typography is unexamined outside of avant-garde media[24]—an argument for an expanded consideration that is overshadowed by the historical presentations and contents of the book. *Typemotion* is an academic instance of the same compendium approach common to graphic design surveys: offering a selection of well-designed and well-animated works that can function as exemplary models for aesthetic consideration. The project originates with the same recognition of *absent* analysis Drucker notes; however, the resulting catalog, although historically illuminating, is not theoretically robust. Their analyses offer a survey that crosscuts both commercial and avant-garde media, presenting a range of applications and examples in which the degree and technology of animation are as important as the results on-screen. The strength of this formal catalog is its breadth, including examples drawn from a wide range of international media that includes TV commercials alongside both video art and feature title sequences. What is missing is a theoretical consideration of motion typography in all these media productions. The identification of animation processes (2D or 3D, interactive or presentational, the problems of ease-in and ease-out, tweening, etc.) or formal elements of typography are not a substitute for the modal, enunciative, and interpretive functions that render meaning through enculturation. This confusion of formal elements with theoretical analysis is common when confronting typography. The heuristics of typographic appearance (the formal issues such as legibility) are not the same as the hermeneutic processes that render signification (the domain of semiotic theory).

Legibility

Modernism emphasizes legibility. Motion graphics inherit this formal concern from graphic design—it develops from the early invention of typography and the printing press, which itself entails a transfer of ideation already in existence.[25] As Canadian media theorist Marshall McLuhan observed: "Typography as the first mechanization of

Typographus. Der Buchdrucker.

ARte mea reliquas illuſtro Typographus artes,
Imprimo dum varios ære micante libros.
Quæ prius aucta ſitu, quæ puluere plena iacebant,
Vidimus obſcura nocte ſepulta premi.

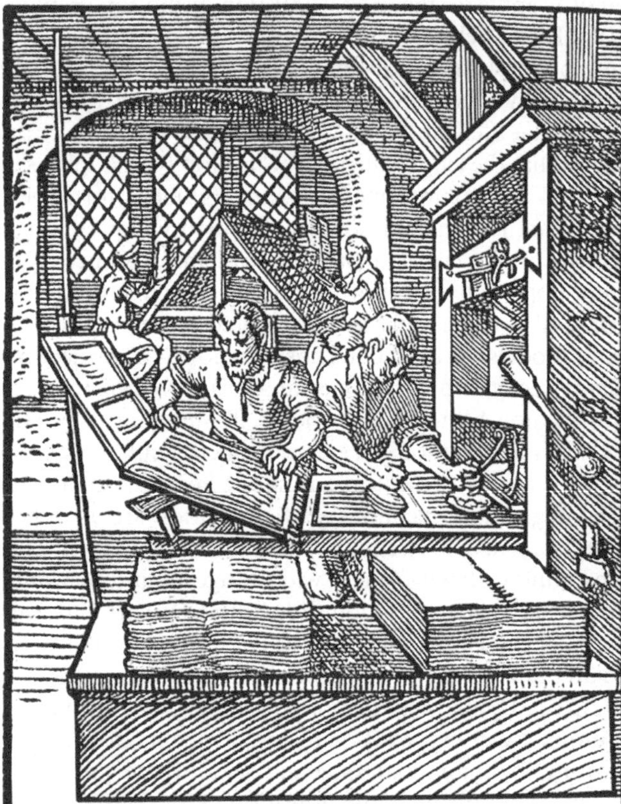

Hæc veterum renouo neglecta volumina Patrum
Atq; ſcolis curo publica facta legi.
Artem prima nouam reperiſſe Moguntia fertur,
Vrbs grauis, & multis ingenioſa modis.
Qua nihil vtilius videt, aut precioſius orbis,
Vix melius quicquam ſecla futura dabunt.

C. 3 Char-

Figure 0.2 "Typographus, Der Buchdrucker" (Typographer, The Printer) from *Das Ständebuch* (*The Book of Trades*, 1568), illustration by Jost Amman (1539–91) and text by Hans Sachs (1494–1576)

handicraft is itself the perfect instance not of a new knowledge, but of applied knowledge."[26] As "printing" became a mechanical process rather than the labor-intensive work of drawing each individual letter, it transformed European society with long-lasting, global impacts: McLuhan's "applied knowledge" does not undermine or alter the cultural significance being produced. Distinctions between reading, language, and writing familiar from design are codified with Johannes Gutenberg's adaptation of a wine press into the first European printing press in 1439, an event that marks a process of technical, machinic evolution and cultural change.[27] However, this invention—*moveable type*—was not an *ex nihilo* development but a changed means of production [Figure 0.2]. It depends on earlier inventions for text, understandings of writing, and conceptions of the 'book' to make its appearance coherent. The book remains stable across the transition created by Gutenberg's invention. Language communicates, the book endures. The use of an existing technical and aesthetic model to direct and manage new production is precisely the definition of a *text-oriented* culture. Yet even as the meaning of 'printing' becomes a technological artifact, the former (manual) activity being renamed 'calligraphy,'[28] the distinctions between visuality and legibility increasingly become significant factors of technological mediation and formal organization—coinciding with the rise of Modernism—rather than artistic caprice.

Anxieties about maintaining legibility are a primary element in Jan Tschichold's *The New Typography* (1926).[29] His theorization is an early proposal in the field of graphic design, reasserted after World War II by Beatrice Warde's anthology on design and typography from 1955, *The Crystal Goblet.* Her analysis, published at the apogee of formalism in the twentieth century, develops the theory of 'invisible typography': text whose metaphoric 'transparency' means typography seems to vanish into a natural lexical recognition, i.e. is maximally *legible*.[30] The potential of typography that *actually* moves is a foreign idea that only appears in metaphoric form. Her concern is with the capacities of printed text to communicate without the design and typography impeding comprehension, a logical application of the 'purity'[31] common to formalist Modernism of the 1950s and 1960s. Written language communicates, thus anything that impedes that process *must* be minimized. Both Warde and Tschichold argue for a reductive process serving the communicative functions of language, but at the same time their use of 'transparency' makes the encultured and learned aspects of lexical engagement disappear (apart from the acquisition of semic knowledge of terms and their uses). These concerns with Modernist legibility delayed the development of motion typography,[32] and have a central place in the historical linkage of Modern design and avant-garde cinema[33] with commercial mass media in the 1950s.[34]

At the moment of this purist dominance, the mid-twentieth century reappraisal of innovations offered by *kinesis* actually began in the 1940s. Graphic designer and impresario Merle Armitage produced a small number of title sequence designs for MGM in 1947,[35] and then discussed his pioneering work with adapting the static innovations of Modern design to cinema. His article for *Print* magazine explored the constraints posed by maximal readability for text-on-screen and its impacts on the organization and design of Hollywood title sequences:

> A book page is generally taller than it is wide, and a book designer becomes accustomed to working with that shape in various dimensions. But the motion picture camera "frame" is wider than it is high, and that makes a considerable difference in the approach to the problem. Even one of the most successful, experienced, and competent men in motion pictures first overlooked the fact that unless the lettering is expanded to the full possible size of the screen frame it will not *carry* to the comparatively remote sections or balconies in large motion picture theaters, and in some of our first attempts in arranging type on the surface of film were interesting, but at a distance unreadable. The necessity to use type in its largest dimension, or to cover the entire available space with lettering, puts the designer in somewhat the position of the singer who must continuously sing at full voice. When all the factors are considered, there seems but a very limited range at the disposal of anyone who elects to keep motion picture titles simple, dignified, and readable.[36]

Being able to read *all* the credits in "the comparatively remote sections or balconies" restricts the design in predictable ways. The primacy of concern with legible typography and visual designs in Armitage's title sequences for *The Hucksters*, *Living in a Big Way*, or *Green Dolphin Street* (all 1947) means there is no attempt to use motion typography—they are essentially filmed, static designs. Historical deployments of motion typography in titles from the 1930s and 1940s are rare; notable designs by animator Walter Lantz in *My Man Godfrey* (1936), *Hold that Ghost* (1941), and *Abbott and Costello Meet Frankenstein* (1948) have the same limited formal concern with legibility that Armitage also employs, but are not Modernist designs. While Lantz's sequences are significantly more active than the static title cards produced by Armitage, his motion typography in *My Man Godfrey* is limited to blinking text. Movement only appears briefly in both designs of the 1940s as animorphs in *Hold that Ghost* and as short disarrangements of elements in *Abbott and Costello Meet Frankenstein*; neither of these animated designs lasts longer than a second because text legibility is the dominant concern in all title sequences made prior to the Designer Period in the 1950s. The visual imagery accompanying the text is conceived as a decoration or enhancement, secondary to its easy readability in even the most distant corner of the theater.

Broadcast design pioneer William Golden, who was the first Creative Director of Advertising and Sales Promotion at CBS-TV in the 1950s, recognized that the material constraints on the recognition and interpretation of on-screen texts extricate motion typography from static composition, declaring it a negative influence on the quality of (Modernist) designs being produced:

> Under the twin impacts of the functionalism of the Bauhaus and the practical demands of American business, the designer was beginning [in the 1930s] to use the combination of word and image to communicate more effectively. Under the influence of modern painters, he became aware (perhaps too aware) of the textural qualities and color values of type as an element of design.[37]

Legibility remains a major issue for typography throughout its history. Approaching the historical developments that Golden adapted to the small screen, TV, however, is complicated by the scope of their banality. Because motion graphics share elements of morphology and structure with the static typography of graphic design, the technological constraints that limited the earliest productions create the illusion that the shared foundation is definitive. Their dynamic relationship, visuality::legibility,[38] creates a range of interpenetrating, mutually exclusive potentials realized by the opposed forms of interpretation *as-image* or *as-language*. While readers fluently shift between these modes, creating an illusion of similarity and masking their differences, they are utterly distinct engagements relying on independent types of established knowledge and interpretive expertise, one linguistic and lexical, the other perceptual and experiential. Armitage's Modernist designs respond to this demand; thus they contain traditionally placed arrangements of simple typefaces in the center of the frame with minimally graphic backgrounds (neutral, with subtle patterns that allowed the typography a maximum of contrast), to ensure a uniform legibility. This concern with legibility (familiar from graphic design, and ascendant in Modernism in the first half of the twentieth century) constrains the size, placement, and design of all on-screen text; the abandonment of this demand for maximal legibility throughout the movie theater marks a major shift in the development of title sequences and prepares for the emergence of the 'reading-image.'

The Post-Modern typographic experiments at the Cranbrook Academy of Art, which abandoned legibility in favor of expressiveness, belong to a questioning of received formal idioms typical of

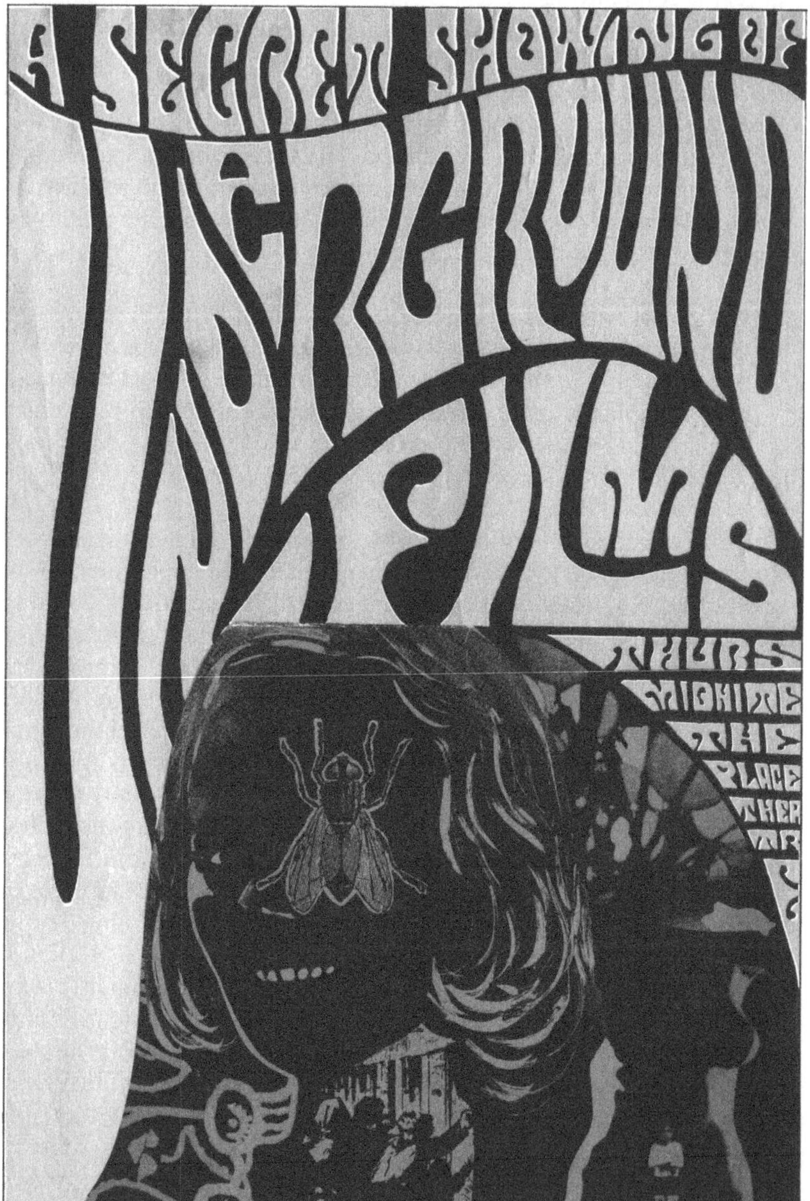

Figure 0.3 Promotional flyer for "A Secret Showing of Underground Films Thurs Midnite The Place Theater," artist uncredited, San Francisco, c. 1968

Post-Modernism that started with the so-called 'psychedelic' posters of the 1960s [Figure 0.3]. Although the approaches taught by Katherine McCoy at Cranbrook in the 1970s and 1980s focused on reintroducing the visuality rejected by the insistence on legibility in design—embracing an expressive formalism (based in post-structural literary theory,[39] or 'typography as discourse')—the established, Modernist paradigms continued to exert an ongoing influence on graphic design outside that school.[40] These formal problematics were identified by Gerhard Bachfischer and Toni Robertson in their discussion "From Movable Type to Moving Type" on the impacts of digital animation:

> On the other extreme, immersion in a typographic performance never happens in book space, it is in fact a different sort of reading experience [...] on one side non-intrusive typography, the invisible art of designing for legibility; on the other side the experience of typographic form, presented in different layers of meaning creating expressions (movement as one of them). When finally the user of a text enters the field, those two sides have to be unified in a holistic approach to reading, in a view that approaches reading as an embedded phenomenon of life, in all its different manifestations.[41]

The concept of "typographic performance" is common to discussion of type in graphic design: it elides the centrality of the audience (the reader) in understanding the work, creating the impression that static type is 'animated' rather than 'presented,' that the 'transformations' created by reading a picture are more than just a metaphor. This distinction becomes important when considering the *kinesis* of motion typography that involves the expressive modulation of actual movement. Bachfischer and Robertson's recognition that typographic performance is a construction is also a revelation of the theoretical vacuum inside design theory arising from its formalist historical engagement. Approaching this particular issue—the ease of reading the text itself (legibility)—as the central problem organized by the material dimensions of the type—such as the relative width, color, size, and optical arrangement—avoids questions about *how* this formal order is at the same time a discourse dependent on past experience and established lexical expertise, which the embracing of post-structural theory by the 'new typography' (such as at Cranbrook) attempted to develop as a formal, expressive praxis.[42]

More recent theorizations of motion and typography take a nuanced approach, recognizing that the addition of motion changes the relationship between legibility and lexical form, distinguishing motion typography from static typography. Barbara Brownie's study *Transforming*

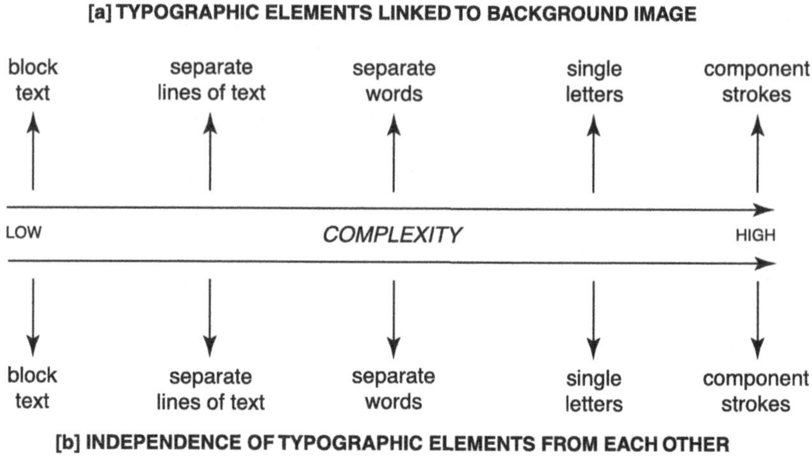

Figure 0.4 Diagram of the two parallel variables in Barbara Brownie's study of motion typography, *Transforming Type*

Type: New Directions in Motion Typography is a notable consideration of animated *kinesis*. Her proposal separates already known and familiar approaches to the organization of typography on the printed page from those on-screen. Brownie's range of *kinesis* includes both graphic 2D animation as well as 3D animation—the full scope of historical uses—offering two high-level variables that each contain the same range of lower-level articulations: [a] describing motions of either individual letterforms or entire words in relation to the background imagery, paralleled by [b] the degree of independence each element or letterform has from the others [Figure 0.4]. Her analysis ably describes the formal orchestration of animated typography to allow it to become a part of the realist 'space' shown on-screen; all the various subtypes she proposes are distinguished by the degree to which the type is 'embedded' in the apparent space of the background imagery. This illusory insertion into the photographic space is a central concern in her analysis, which argues against the presumptive foundations of typography in graphic design—that letterforms themselves are stable. The emergent and animated aspects of motion typography are fluid, offering deformations and ambiguity:

> There is an assumption that the properties of individual letterforms should remain constant, as they would in print.[43]

The changing and unstable nature of typographic materials (letterforms) in motion graphics destabilizes the foundations of graphic design and illuminates the basic difference that *kinesis* makes for typography: where the printed page is static and cannot develop or change its arrangement or legibility, for motion graphics these shifting relationships between familiar letterforms and unfamiliar shapes does not undermine the integrity of the text nor impede its comprehension for the viewer, creating instead unique semantics offered by motion *for* typography. The Modernist dominance of legibility as an essential criterion is never put into question; theorizations of motion typography and motion graphics generally are hindered by traditional assumptions derived from the stability of the printed page. The established parameters of graphic design do not continue to apply in the same ways or with the familiar results for lexical form when they are translated into the field of motion pictures. These distinctions become apparent through the role that time—the chronology of presentation—has in the articulation and interpretation of motion typography: the 'reading-image' develops from the shifting positions, arrangement, and legibility of what appears on-screen. These additional dimensions for lexical forms change the role that audience perceptions have in their understanding. Unlike static graphics and typography, *kinesis* and the 'reading-image' return to aesthetic and conceptual issues originating in the use of text and typography as vehicles of expression beyond their lexical form in the so-called 'silent film.' This early film history is immanent in motion typography, making its analysis in terms of *cinema* not only appropriate, but a needed corrective to the restrictive, fallacious influence of graphic design on its theorization and development.

The Technical Lineage

Technologies do not anticipate their future uses beyond the parameters of their initial construction-development, but they do retain the traces of the earlier technologies that informed their invention. This connection to the past makes the new machine familiar in its relationship to what it supplants and replaces, no matter how different it actually is; the concept of 'disruptive technology' describes internalized relationships that apply to both contemporary digital technologies and the historical impacts of new technologies on the traditional arts.[44] Philosopher Bernard Stiegler's work on *technics* connects these developments to their cultural-historical foundations:

> The technical essence is the identity of the lineage, its family resemblance, the specificity of its patrimony, which is the secret of its singular becoming: 'The technical essence is recognized in the fact that it remains stable through the evolutional lineage, and not only stable, but productive as well of structures and functions by internal development and progressive saturation.'[45]

Stiegler's process naturalizes innovations created by industrialization, leading to the contemporary 'hyperindustrial era,' where human memory and knowledge become part of the productive apparatus (the digital computer) and which the 'reading-image' visualizes.[46] Of particular concern to his proposal are media such as sound recording or cinema; the ability to return to and 'relive' recorded experiences depends on how these technical apparati convert (externalize) memory as immanent, repeatable experience.[47] He argues that the audience for these recordings can have a new experience of the same memory since "this gives rise to the *not-yet*; that the already-heard gives way to the not-yet-heard, echoing a protentional expectation."[48] As with relistening to a record played on a gramophone or a digital recording on a cell phone, these experiences depend precisely on the technical ability to replay a recording, the repetition that brings 'past' experience into the present. Audience anticipation can then direct interpretation in listening to/playing a recording, so that memory creates a higher-level order for what happens and how it is engaged. Thus the technical capacity—recording sounds and images—expands upon the established capacity of *text* to externalize abstract information and knowledge; the proposition of 'reading-image' mediates between these two varieties of recording and experiential encapsulation to model the recognition–interpretation process back to its audience, externalizing those internal shifts literally on-screen. Not all motion typography always creates this visualization of interpretation; however, the *potential* is sufficient to separate the category of motion typography from its relatives in static design.

Understanding the lineage of motion graphics' development from simple hand-animation into the contemporary digital computer's automation/simulation of earlier technologies offers a critical opportunity to acknowledge the role of the apparatus as not only instrumentality but ideology. Technical evolution progressively renders the machinic impacts invisible, as ideological forces make it into the natural order which enables the next series of innovations and refinements. At the same time, these changes are an exteriorization of remembered experiences as the repeatable (and often repeated) imageosphere of mediation and its digital re/distribution. The contemporary challenges[49] posed by digital computers (also known as "post-cinema"[50]) and the material conversion of all moving imagery into a plastically transformable field[51] following the metastable model of animation[52]—based in a new degree of control over the "atomistic" capacity of animation to transform anything appearing on-screen[53]—makes the centrality of this technical lineage for motion graphics into a means to theorize motion typography and the 'reading-image.'

TITLE DESIGN IN HOLLYWOOD FILMS[54]	
Early (Experimental) Period	(beginning until ~1915)
Silent Period	(until ~1927)
Studio Period	(until ~1955)
Designer Period	(until ~1977)
Logo Period	(until ~1995)
Contemporary Designer Period	(1995 to present)

This periodization of feature film title sequences reflects shifts in both technology and aesthetics, enabling a consideration separate from the particulars of typography's *narrative* and *crediting functions*. Animation processes emerge in technological as well as aesthetic limitations on the designs possible, but these inventions pose a fundamental challenge for any consideration of the link between aesthetics and motion picture technology, as film historian Raymond Fielding explains:

> There is a temptation for film historians in particular to interpret the development of the motion picture teleologically, as if each generation of workers had sketched out the future of the art far in advance of the technology required for its realization. In fact, however, the artistic evolution of the film has always been intimately associated with technological change, just as it has, in less noticeable fashion, in the older arts. Just as the painter's art has changed with the introduction of different media and processes, just as the forms of symphonic music have developed with the appearance of new kinds of instruments, so has the elaboration and refinement of film style followed from the introduction of more sophisticated machinery. [...] If the artistic and historical development of film and television are to be understood, then so must the peculiar marriage of art and technology which prevails in their operation.[55]

In considering the historical periods of feature film titles, the role of technology becomes obvious as a determinant and a constant refrain in the aesthetic development these periods identify; however, all innovations are proximate, created for immediate and specific problems confronting the filmmakers, not out of a desire to create a *future* aesthetic. Each new method and machinery achieves success and general adoption not because of an aesthetic capacity, but because it enables already known kinds of production to become faster, cheaper, and more precise than other, existing (and competing) technologies: it is a question of cost, since motion pictures are a business, conducted for profit.

Although most familiar from the feature film title sequence, the history of animated typography as it emerged in motion pictures is complex. New technologies have not added new aesthetic potentials for the 'reading-image'; there have been no new types of *kinetic action*, *graphic expression*, and *chronic progression* to accompany the introduction of new, digital tools. Instead, new technologies have enabled the development of greater complexity and ease of production for what were formerly difficult processes, making them accessible and common. These technical and aesthetic sources for motion typography are apparent in how avant-garde film was transformed into a commercial, banal product by its audiences in the advertising industry.[56]

Motion typography aligns with the historical periods of feature film title design, but remains separate, a parallel trajectory whose technical and stylistic lineage also appears in title sequences. Although the animation and integration of typography with background photography has always been a technical possibility since the earliest motion pictures, the use and organization of complex, highly animated text-on-screen remained a relative rarity prior to the development of digital computers. Stiegler observed that the technical object maintains a family resemblance where each successive generation provides a "natural technical evolution" that involves the synthesis of earlier machineries—whether the book, printing press, motion picture, or digital computer—into a new instrumentality. Motion graphics are defined by this historical *lineage* of animation techniques merged with typographic conventions. Despite technological changes, improvements, and revolutions, only four approaches to on-screen design with motion typography have emerged over its century of development: [a] as filmed, static design; [b] as type overlay composited with photography; [c] as a simultaneous orchestration of type and photography to create a unitary design (the focus of Brownie's analysis); [d] type in/as animation integrated with background imagery. The 'reading-image' may appear in any of these technical approaches since it defines *not* the formal arrangement of materials, but a particular way of using them to model the progression of interpretive thought and the lexical recognition of on-screen text.

Fielding concluded the fourth edition of his extensive study *The Technique of Special Effects Cinematography* (published in 1984) with a brief discussion anticipating the future: the potential impacts of digital technology. The optical printer's capacity to reconstruct, reshape, and selectively reproduce parts of the already sampled motions of kinematography was an invention with far-reaching impacts. This ability to transform the recorded motions of a film definitively removed it from the realm of a difficult-to-alter 'document' created by a machine, to a plastic and fluidly alterable construction familiar from more traditional art. His prescient discussion makes the connection between historical technologies and contemporary digital systems explicit, revealing it as a foundational part of their technical design:

> There is no question that the introduction and perfection of an electronic optical printer could theoretically revolutionize the process of composite cinematography and optical printing. In addition to all of the capabilities of a modern optical printer, such a system could be able to enhance photographic images, minimize grain, add color to black-and-white images or alter colors radically, multiply image elements to whatever extent desired, correct over- and underexposure, and remove scratches or wires from within the picture area. It is even theoretically possible that such a device could separate designated foreground details out of the background without the need for blue-screen backings, and that computer software could be designed to accomplish this, more-or-less automatically, with a minimum of human instruction. With such a system, the images of expensive miniatures, set pieces, props, crowds, water and sky scenes, and the like might be 'stockpiled' and retrieved at will for use in new films! In theory, at least, all things are possible with such a system.[57]

Fielding's "electronic optical printer" matches the capacities of contemporary digital compositing software precisely.[58] Historically specialized photographic and rephotographic processes are the common progenitor of both motion graphics and visual effects—the ability to alter, combine, and manipulate multiple images into a singular, seamless unit. This technical development is a refinement of earlier processes which it displaced. While optical printing was more expensive than the superimposition process of 'B-roll,' introduced by photographer Fred Archer while he was Director of Art Titles at Universal Pictures between 1919 and 1925, it offered a greater range of options for beginning the film, making its dominance in motion graphics entirely predictable. The transformation and automation of optical printing with computer technology is a change and refinement of technology, not a revolution in aesthetics. These relations become apparent in how digital tools are transformative for motion typography. By enabling the automation of the tedious, mechanical parts of animation, the digital computer has proved especially capable of animating typography and design on-screen; the four design approaches to *kinesis* remain constant as high-level orderings that are independent of the methods of their production. Technologies used to create moving typography were *not* invented for that purpose alone—more often it is one capability included with other, more immediately necessary ones, as was the case with the optical printer. This precision animation camera, designed for direct rephotography of motion picture film by cinematographer Linwood Dunn in 1929, was initially employed for the production of visual effects; that the same technology of masks and rephotography could also be employed for creating dynamic title sequences was simply a bonus that quickly found application in title sequences, compositing typography over live action footage.

Animation has been a central part of the title sequence's production throughout its history, a link between visual form and typography that creates motion graphics as a field.[59] However, the changing material constraints on the extent and application of animation's techniques in title design are revealed by changes between periods for feature film titles in the United States: the shift from short films to features in 1915, as the Silent Period began, was both a technological change as well as an aesthetic expansion; the embracing of synchronized sound, starting in 1927, and optical printing two years later (in 1929) marks the start of the Studio Period; the challenges posed by television in the 1950s led to the beginning of the Designer Period; the eventual embracing of TV and video in the 1970s led to the emergence of the Logo Period in the 1980s; and digital production produced a convergence of film and TV titling in the Contemporary Period. The introduction of electronic and digital tools for television in the 1980s, including but not limited to broadcast-ready technologies such as the *Quantel Paintbox* and much cheaper consumer technologies (what were termed 'prosumer') such as the *Fairlight CVI* or *NewTek Video Toaster*, both employed the same conceptions of generative text-on-screen as the earlier on-film technologies they emulated. These systems are the ancestors to the "electronic optical printer" that Fielding described in his conclusion: the simulation of optical printing on the digital computer in software such as *Adobe AfterEffects* combines the discrete technologies of on-film production and the compositing, processing, and generating of the television studio in a hybrid system that has replaced its progenitors. In each case new technology offers not only different methods of production, but also radical reductions in costs that eliminate earlier restrictions limiting use. The four approaches to design do not change; only the frequency and extent of their use in motion graphics varies.

Arranging the four design approaches in chronological order of emergence attests to their linked foundations and evolutional lineage. The earliest approach is also the simplest: using type as a graphic element by filming text or a design with both pictures and text using an animation stand. It is the closest that motion graphics ever comes to being 'filmed graphic design.' This essential historical basis in animation—the sequential photographing of individual elements—expands through combination with photography to create the more familiar composited (or simply superimposed) figure–ground relationship where text and image coexist in parallel on-screen. Type overlay—whether produced

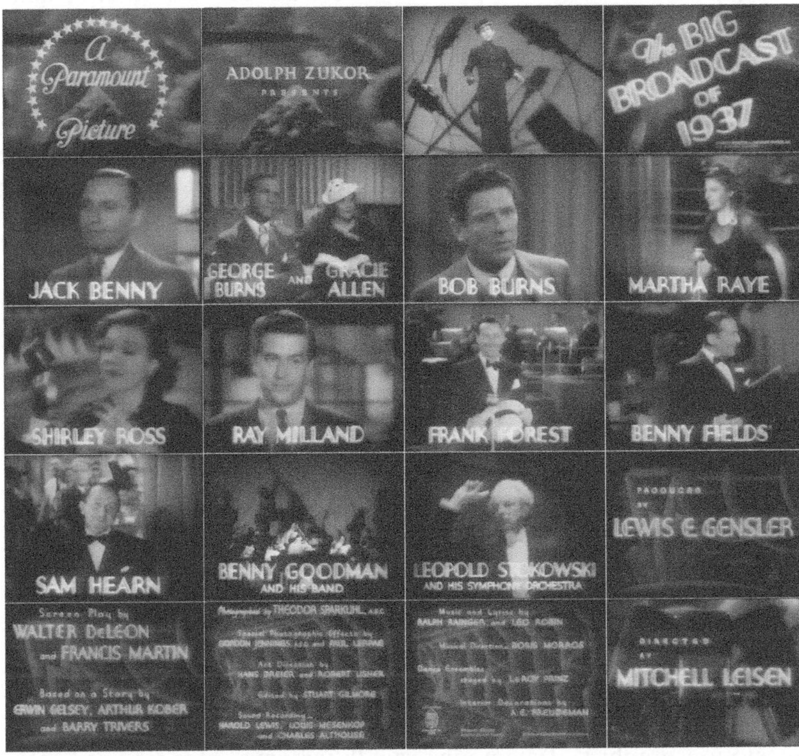

Figure 0.5 All the title cards in the title sequence for *The Big Broadcast of 1937* (1936)

using Archer's B-roll superimposition process or with an optical printer or digital computer—remains essentially the same: the three modes of understanding text–image composites emerge alongside the first such composites produced in the 1920s. The figure–ground mode, calligram mode, and rebus mode that link the interpretations of text and image remain constant over time. In the titles for *The Big Broadcast of 1937* (1936) [Figure 0.5] optical printing creates the calligrams that introduce each actor—their name appears below their portrait. The coordination of photography and typography is a specific development that initially complicates the superimposition of text over a background image, but is also a logical development of it: coordinating both text and photography, apparent in Steven Frankfurt's title sequence for *To Kill A Mockingbird* (1962), unifies the live action events of the photography with changes in crediting, and its influence evolves into the use of visual effects techniques to apparently embed the text within the live action background, allowing the type to respond to and interact with it. Digital technology enabled this convergence of live action and animation with the parallel use of text in/as animation. The transformation of typography, where the letterforms become graphics in themselves, privileges the visual over the lexical and is common to designs as diverse and otherwise utterly different as the art titles in F. A. A. Dahme's *Dance Macabre* (1921) and Terry Gilliam's animations for *Life of Brian* (1979). These integrations of titling into imagery serve to anticipate the digital embedding of text with the pictorial environment; the digital convergence of live action and animation makes these types of fusion not only common but inexpensive. However, this combination also means that these 'new' applications and integrations were pioneered decades earlier, minimizing their genuine novelty. The continuity between physical technical approaches and the generation of titles and graphics with a digital computer makes this technical lineage especially important for understanding motion typography. The continuity of the 'reading-image' throughout this history validates the importance of considering 'antique' rather than contemporary works.

Typography and Titling

The historical development of 'on-screen text' in early cinema established the parameters for the development of motion typography in the title sequence, a framework that continues to structure its interpretive modes in motion graphics. Typography rapidly assumed standardized roles, easily identified and understood by viewers. The functions and importance of art titles for narrative cinema during the 1910s and 1920s, prior to the commercial success of synchronized sound recording, were not merely a feature of the use of decorative backgrounds, but an articulation of cadence and suggestions of delivery made through the stylization and appearance of the letterforms themselves.

The historical sources of contemporary motion typography inform its complexity and enunciative form: familiar expressive functions are apparent in the use of Expressionist title cards in Robert Weine's film *The Cabinet of Dr. Caligari* (1919) that anticipates later developments, both in type design and in their integration with the narrative as a presentation of character subjectivity.[60] The influence of this film is pervasive, if not always apparent; it is paradigmatic, neither irrelevant nor ignorable in the later evolutional lineage of on-screen typography. Considering its dynamics is therefore warranted given its direct influence in the United States. Author and critic Gilbert Seldes's discussion of American avant-garde films in *The New Republic* in March 1929 identified the importance of *The Cabinet of Dr. Caligari* as a reference point in the consideration of film productions and the initial proposition of 'film art':

> "*The Last Moment*," by Dr. Paul Fejos, also lay outside the professional field and, although it seemed to me a silly and ineffective pastiche of all the superficial mannerisms of all the art-films of America and Germany, it achieved a similar success [to Robert Florey's film *The Life and Death of 9413*] for its director. Finally J. S. Watson and Melville Weber have produced "*The Fall of the House of Usher.*" According to the magazine *Movie Makers*, the January [1929] issue of which should be read by all interested in the subject, Mr. Wilton Barrett, secretary of the National Board of Review, has said that this picture represents "the greatest advance made in the progress of the motion picture as an independent art since that epochal film, '*The Cabinet of Dr. Caligari.*'" [...] The amateurs simplify when they do not discard story-content (Dr. Watson says "the amateur can use [a story] if it helps him think"); they are opposed to naturalism; they have no stars; they are over-influenced by "*Caligari*"—the commercial directors are still under-influenced by the same film—they want to give their complete picture without the aid of any medium except the camera and projector.[61]

What Seldes calls "amateur" is based on the economics of production, rather than aesthetics—the resources and technical capacities of a commercial movie studio are greater than what the "amateur" has available for their more modest productions. However, his comments do illustrate the centrality of *The Cabinet of Dr. Caligari* to the aesthetic considerations of 'film art.' Its Expressionist morphology and progression are the salient features for consideration: the manipulation and transformation of visible reality in the narrative to render a subjective interpretation rather than a passive rendition of a seemingly familiar realism. The status given to *The Cabinet of Dr. Caligari* in the 1920s would wane by the late 1930s, as Harold Leonard, editor of *The Film Index* compiled by the Museum of Modern Art, states regarding its influences on cinema in the United States:

> But the American film had made little progress with its critics despite these minor gains when *The Cabinet of Dr. Caligari* arrived from Germany in 1921. Merely the first in a train of bizarre, somber, and tendentious productions from that country, it set up an "arty," anti-Hollywood orientation in serious film criticism which was to hinder the advance of true standards for almost a decade.[62]

His rejection of Expressionism is a reversal of the value given to it by Seldes, but retains the same recognitions of subjectivity presented on-screen: his rejection depends on how *The Cabinet of Dr. Caligari* deviates from the realist expectations posed by the other narrative films produced by the Hollywood film studios. The "true standards" he describes are apparent in the realist use of synchronized sound and naturalistic presentations that became common in the studio productions of the 1930s as typography on-screen became progressively more inessential to narrative. The naturalistic realism of studio productions is an aesthetic opposed to any Expressionist, clearly fabricated visual style. These mutually exclusive views distinguish the outmost positions in the range of naturalism::stylization that come to define the realist aesthetics employed in Hollywood studio productions, with the relative de/valuation of *The Cabinet of Dr. Caligari* serving as an immediate means to identify partisanship within this 'debate' over the appropriate ways to manage and present the mediation inherent to motion pictures.

Questions about mediation, rather than being extraneous to the role of text-on-screen and the consideration of typography's expressive dimensions, illuminate the 'reading-image' and interpretive significance beyond lexical presentation.[63] The greater debates between an aesthetic realism of surface and familiar appearances, and a realism guided by and presenting a subjective, mental reality meant that more subtle questions were neglected or ignored. The dynamics of text::image, and the consideration of graphic modeling or animated arrangement, were causalities of partisan conflicts over basic aesthetic issues: it is difficult to attend to subtleties when the foundations of motion images are in question.

The periodization of motion picture title sequences in the United States provides a framework to identify these aesthetic transformations and how they impact motion typography over the course of the twentieth century. The contemporary distinction between those titles that provide crediting for the actors and production personnel, and the internal titles of narrative enunciation that to contemporary viewers seem absolute and unquestionable was not always so distinct. The separation of intertitles from crediting is a separation of functions that emerged gradually; it is an example of the rationalizations of motion picture form—standardization—that accompany the dominance of the Hollywood studio system, where movies are produced as an industrial commodity following the model of the assembly line, with compartmentalized tasks and strictly separated roles and functions in manufacturing.

However, during the Silent Period there was a greater complexity and fluidity of functions for typography on-screen, giving the role of visuality a prominent position in on-screen typographic aesthetics. The debate for and against the aesthetic value of *The Cabinet of Dr. Caligari*'s Expressionism[64] did not have the urgency or polarization during this period that it would gain in the 1930s after the commercial success and general adoption of synchronized sound recording. The 'reading-image' employs these same graphic and animated dimensions of typography for expressive purposes—appropriate for designs influenced by German Expressionism[65]—informing the multiplicity of functions that arise in response to the informational, dramatic, and interpretive demands of a cinema made without the assistance of spoken language. Historian Brad Chisholm proposed a series of roles for Silent Period typography in "Reading Intertitles." He discussed their role prior to a general reduction in and, in many cases, elimination of on-screen text in the decades that followed. His study concerns "expository intertitles": those texts appearing on-screen that perform *narrative functions*. The seven categories he proposes mirror similar functions performed in literature, suggesting an understanding of narrative cinema as a type of complex, live action picture book that makes the relevance of lexical structures learned in early childhood appropriate for understanding the dynamics of text-on-screen, such as the calligram mode.[66] Chisholm explains the importance of on-screen typography for the Silent Period as an essential part of these films' narrative organization:

> Most people agree there are two broad categories of intertitles: *dialogue* intertitles—those enunciated within the diegesis, set off by quotation marks; and *expository* intertitles—those enunciated outside the diegesis. [...] During the late teens and early 1920s Hollywood filmmakers relied more heavily on expository intertitles than on dialogue intertitles. [...] The descendants of expository intertitles can still be found in the films of today, and several of the old functions are frequently handled via the printed word. It is common to superimpose the place name or a temporal marker over the first establishing shot in a film or after a major narrative transition. Scrolling expository summaries often opened Hollywood films in the 1930s and 1940s, "Chapter Headings" are sometimes used for purposes of nostalgia, and numerous films weave their opening credits well into the texture of their action. Occasionally a sound-era [Studio Period] film will use a legitimate old-fashioned intertitle. Such an intertitle cannot claim quite the same status as its forbears, however. Now that synchronized sound is the norm, every use of an intertitle functions as a commentary on the discourse.[67]

Chisholm's seven categories of titling are distinguished by their *narrative function*: [a] *identifications* that serve to credit actors; [b] *temporal markers* that relay information about time and place; [c] *narrative summary* that relays backstory; [d] *characterization* that explains motives or feelings; [e] *mediated thoughts/paraphrased dialogue* that reveal internal monologues; and [f] *commentary* on what is happening in the story or scene being shown; [g] the seventh category (which Chisholm does not consider) is *dialogue*. The integral nature of intertitles for the silent films he considers does not extend to their graphic or visual character. The visuality of the *type* (and thus the 'reading-image') are not factors in his analysis. The sample texts presented in his discussion are all designed for maximal legibility—the text is an essentially undecorated typeface with a slight serif, common and familiar from books and magazines to the point of being almost generic in its impact: the text is 'transparent' and offers no explicit additional commentary on the meaning of the words than their presentation to-be-read. This 'invisible typography' (described by Warde) is a normative engagement where the audience's acceptance of enunciations understands the lexical as conveying the entirety of the meaning. However, the ability of different audience members to see the same thing, yet interpret it in radically different ways, demonstrates how audience interpretations grow deeper and more complex through repeated encounters with new examples.[68] Past experience allows viewers to parse their perceptions into coherence, as well as enabling them to anticipate and recognize divergences from established norms.[69] Eco's theorization of 'serial form' makes this 'transparency' a product of how past experience is central to audience interpretation: it is the recognition and assignment of meaning to familiar forms, as well as the capacity to adapt to unfamiliar and neologistical arrangements. The body of knowledge an audience *already* has before their encounter with any particular work delimits the ways viewers will understand and interpret that work to create, for example, the narrative/dramatic relationships of outcome and consequence that are fundamental to (narrative) comprehension:

> What is more interesting is when the quotation is explicit and recognizable, as happens in post-modern literature and art, which blatantly and ironically play on the intertextuality [...] aware of the quotation, the spectator is brought to elaborate ironically on the nature of such a device and to acknowledge the fact that one has been invited to play upon one's encyclopedic knowledge.[70]

Recognizing quotations is fundamentally an issue of historical knowledge applied in the immanent encounter. Audiences are active, drawing on their established 'past experience' to recognize morphology and structure, actions to separate the text from the other visual material that define 'fluency' and inform its relationships with the other materials on-screen. Chisholm's analysis of the typographic functions created in these quotational uses is schematic and limited. His denial of the graphic aspects of the text is simultaneously unsurprising and shocking; however, a refusal to acknowledge the graphic expressiveness is to be expected given the focus of his discussion: D. W. Griffith's film *Broken Blossoms* only has very simple, legible text. At the same time the lack of recognition for the expressive role of typography in early films, ranging from *The Cabinet of Dr. Caligari* to Walter Anthony's text layouts in *The Cat and The Canary* (1927), ignores how letters dramatize not only the words but their importance. This refusal recalls the debates over naturalism::stylization that define the realist presentation of 'subjectivity' and 'objectivity' in cinema, and the tendency to focus on narrative functions of cinema to the exclusion of all else both enforce the neglect of typography.

Chisholm's analysis makes the continuity of roles for the 'reading-image' in the 'silent film' and later sync-sound productions obvious. The shift in function to being a commentary on the discourse happens precisely because of the ways that text becomes an independent feature of the motion picture, rather than an integral part of its narrational progression. This shift reflects the same distinctions that separate the 'title sequence' from the other sequences that follow, a pseudo-independent self-containment defined by the centrality of text-on-screen to the credits. Only in rare instances, such as the film *Scott Pilgrim vs. the World* (2010) directed by Edgar Wright, are typography and graphics a constant and continuous element within the narrative, performing a central role in *narrative function*. The superficially familiar world appearing on-screen is one filled with and interpenetrated by texts, along with graphics from video games (the score of "1,000" that appears after "Scott Pilgrim" (played by Michael Cera) defeats the first "Evil Ex" he encounters) and visualizations familiar from comic books (the "SHHHH" and graphics expressing emotion) appear within the diegesis [Figure 0.6]. While the animated sounds are beyond the scope of Chisholm's taxonomy, the more traditionally presented texts, even when they are drawn from video games, are not. They are "added to the image"[71] in a way that is entirely different than the texts that appear on signs, painted on walls, or elsewhere in the diegetic 'space,' yet they are simultaneously *of* that space and are understood by the audience in precisely the same ways that those texts physically present during filming are, being visibly embedded within the visual space of these characters' world (diegetic). Thus, while these typo/graphics function as exposition, at the same time they are features of that visual space, presumably something the characters in the film are aware of and respond to, not merely non-diegetic or extra-diegetic visualizations for the benefit of the audience.

The narrative is a highly realistic fantasy that only seemingly resembles the familiar world of everyday experience. The 'rating' that appears next to (and behind) "Scott Pilgrim" early in the film acts as both an *identification* of the character as "22 Years Old" and a brief *commentary* on him as "awesome." Yet this statement about him has an ambivalent character: it can be read as *external* (as a statement of fact) or *internal* (as a self-expression of the character) depending on how this text is understood in relation to the diegesis. Initially there may be

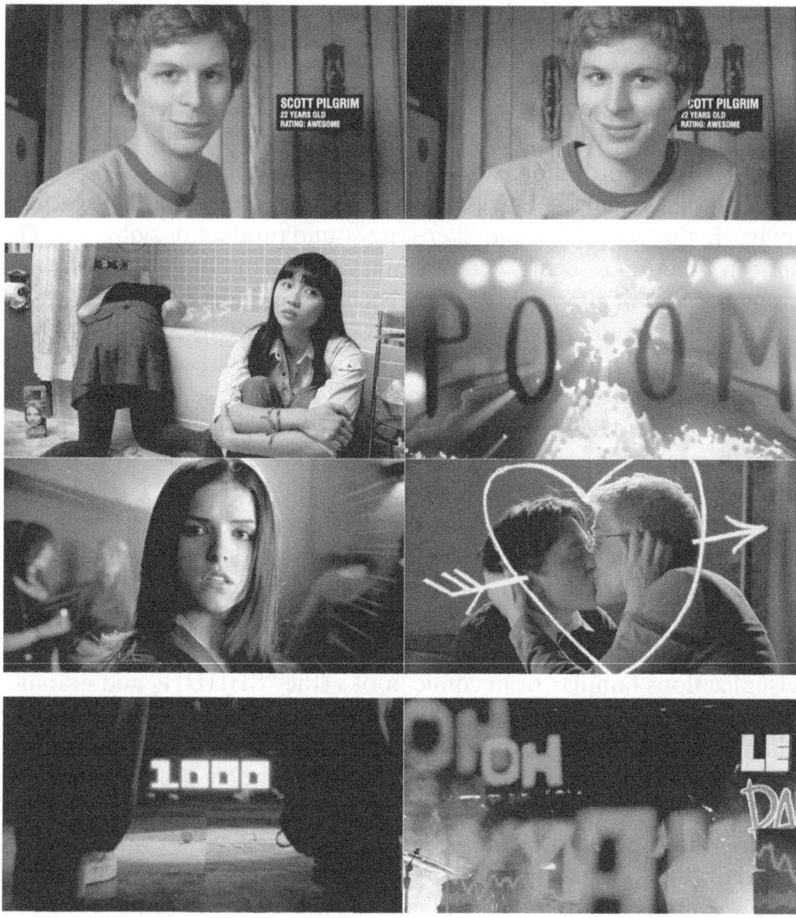

Figure 0.6 Selected stills from *Scott Pilgrim vs. the World* (2010), showing examples of integrated typography and graphics within the diegesis

uncertainty about whether the text/graphics are features of this world or simply elements shown to the viewer; as this initial scene progresses, it becomes apparent that these visuals are contiguous with the rest of the screen-world, not just artfully presented non-diegetic elements such as subtitles. Their integration collapses the comfortable distinctions between crediting/titling and photographic imagery to challenge the separation of naturalism::stylization. These transgressions of typical cinematic realism reveal the role of text in narrative cinema is more fluid than Chisholm's commentary suggests: the *identification* performed by this rating can only be accepted as discourse about the narrative if its embedded nature is ignored, since to integrate it with the diegesis suggests that "Scott Pilgrim" is *not* 'awesome' in a positive sense, but rather narcissistic and perhaps self-deluding about his own 'awesomeness,' both points of self-knowledge for this character that define his 'character arc.'

The Expressionist character of the other texts that serve as illustrations—as with the dramatization of the lyrics "Oh Yeah" or the video game score—includes the onomatopoetic animated sound/graphics. These elements appear prominently on-screen and are understood as integral to the environment, visualizing essential parts of what happens. This *narrative function* reinforces their integration without the ambivalence of Scott's rating. Only the category that Chisholm does not develop, *dialogue*, offers the possibility of accommodating these presentations: they are visual statements that cannot *only* be attributed to the characters (although there are instances where they are linked to a character as 'dialogue'). Acting as intrusions into the otherwise familiar realism, each element serves as a dramatization whose shifting relationship to the events is masked by its diegetic linkage *illustrating* each shot. This role anchors the text in the diegesis, acting as a motion graphic analogue to Drucker's proposal of 'navigation' as a manipulation of graphics and compositions at the level of discourse and presentation:

> Readings of narrative texts rarely include attention to the graphic devices that structure presentation in print or electronic formats. These devices are rendered invisible by habits of reading. But, I would suggest, these graphic elements do more than structure the conditions in which narration is produced. By their hierarchy, arrangement, organization and other features they contribute to the production of the narrative in substantive ways.[72]

The text/graphics of *Scott Pilgrim vs. the World* are not just visual decorations: the text stating "Oh Yeah" is more than merely a rendering of the sung lyrics, it also mirrors the dialogue between "Scott Pilgrim" and "Ramona Flowers" (played by Mary Elizabeth Winstead), visualizing her non-verbal responses as the "Oh Yeah" text—anticipating who the next "Evil Ex" is—and rendering Scott's "Oh No" directly comical. The set-up of text, dialogue, and visualization creates a dynamic where understanding the joke in this scene depends on the recognition of these words' duplicity as an enthusiastic agreement *and* recognition of dread. This text behaves as an Expressionist *performance* that draws attention to Scott's realization of imminent disaster. The climactic moment of *The Cabinet of Dr. Caligari* [Figure 0.7] employs text in a similar role, not as dialogue but as a diegetic expression or dramatization showing

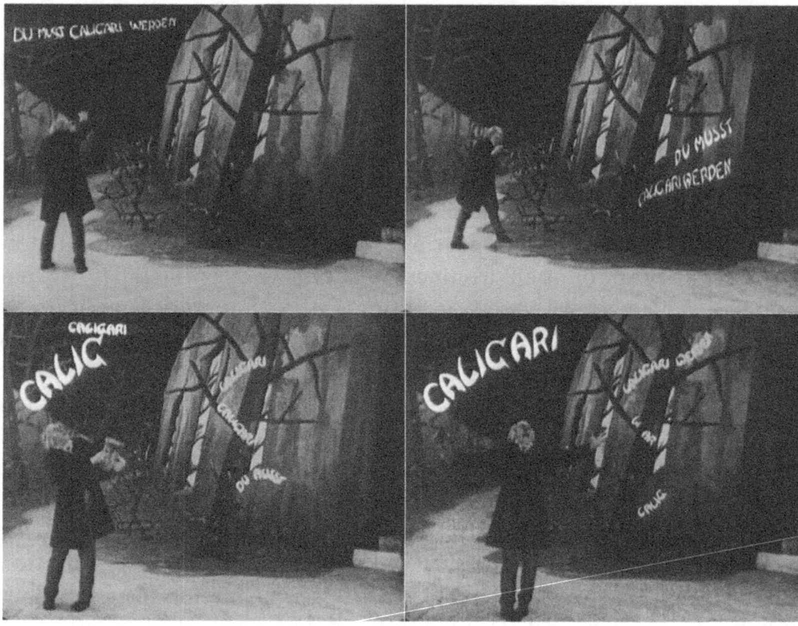

Figure 0.7 Stills stating "DU MUSST CALIGARI WERDEN" ("YOU MUST BECOME CALIGARI") from *The Cabinet of Dr. Caligari* (1919), showing extra-diegetic typography

the emergent insanity of insane asylum director "Dr. Caligari" (played by Werner Krauss), which the audience understands through the interaction of performance and texts appearing on-screen as an unreal but immanent part of the diegesis (thus, extra-diegetic).[73] The narration evident in both motion pictures converges in the same articulation of Expressionist visuality where the text has an excess of signification beyond its syntactic meaning—i.e. a 'reading-image.' This 'reading-image' interaction of narrative context and its on-screen morphology is more than the sum of each element in itself. For *The Cabinet of Dr. Caligari* the knowledge is tragedy; in *Scott Pilgrim vs. The World* it is farce. That these dimensions of typo/graphics are commonly ignored as part of embracing of an idealized, 'transparent' lexical engagement responds to the same systemic denials of stylization in favor of naturalism that elide the importance of *The Cabinet of Dr. Caligari* for the complex articulations of motion pictures generally.

The appeal of 'opacity' in understanding these developments of typo/graphics lies with the difficult heritage of a dominant Modernist approach that ignores and denies the critical interest of hybrids and intermedia forms, historically resulting in the 'reading-image' remaining unacknowledged. In considering it as a vehicle of articulation and thus a model for understanding typography in media, conceiving of motion typography as 'peripheral' becomes a serious critical fallacy. The orchestration of text, graphics, images, and sounds in motion graphics offers the capacity to consider those precise relations where typography becomes more than merely lexical—its role in cinema implicitly informs the range of realist forms in commercial media. The 'reading-image' invokes interpretive modes (*kinetic action*, *graphic expression*, and *chronic progression*), mediating boundaries and expressions created in and by motion pictures to differentiate motion graphics from the static approaches of graphic design through the central role of *kinesis*.

Notes

1 Schellong, M. "Moving Signs: Playing with Legibility and Aesthetic Experience" *Typemotion* ed. Bernd Scheffer, Christine Stenzer, Peter Weibel and Soenke Zehle (Karlsruhe: Hatje Cantz/ZKM, 2015) pp. 55–57.
2 Scheffer, B. and Stenzer, C., eds. *Schriftfilme: Schrift als Bild in Bewegung* (Bielefeld: Aisthesis, 2009).
3 Halas, J. *Graphics in Motion: From the Special Effects Film to Holographics* (New York: Van Norstrand Reinhold Co., 1984).
4 Brown, D. "The AIGA Medalist 1981: Saul Bass" *AIGA Graphic Design USA:3 The Annual of the American Institute of Graphic Arts* (New York: Watson-Guptill Publications, 1981) pp. 13–44.
5 Shaw, A. *Design for Motion* (New York: Focal Press, 2016).
6 Drucker, J. "What is a Word's Body?" *What is? Nine Epistemological Essays* (Victoria: Cuneform Press, 2013) p. 38.
7 Wainer, H. "Preface to the 2010 edition of the English Translation" *Semiology of Graphics* trans. William J. Berg (Redlands: Esri Press, 2010) pp. xi–xii.
8 Jakobson, R. "On the Verbal Art of William Blake and other Poet-Painters" *Linguistic Inquiry* vol. 1, no. 1. (January, 1970) pp. 3–23.
9 Might have proposed, but didn't: the 'reading image' in *Vision, Image, Record: A Cultivation of the Visual Field* (Antony Fredriksson, Åbo Akademi University Press, 2014) is entirely different, based in narrative concerns; see pp. 149–153.
10 Betancourt, M. *Title Sequences as Paratexts: Narrative Anticipation and Recapitulation* (New York: Routledge Focus, 2018).
11 Metz, C. *Impersonal Enunciation, or the Place of Film* trans. Corman Deane (New York: Columbia University Press, 2015) pp. 46–51.
12 Ramsaye, T. *A Million and One Nights* (New York: Simon & Schuster, 1924).
13 Bardèche, M. and Brasillach, R. *The History of Motion Pictures* (New York: Norton, 1938).
14 Jacobs, L. *The Rise of the American Film* (New York: Harcourt, Brace and Company, 1939/1948).

15 Betancourt, M. *Semiotics and Title Sequences: Text–Image Composites in Motion Graphics* (New York: Routledge Focus, 2017).
16 Metz, C. *Impersonal Enunciation, or the Place of Film* trans. Corman Deane (New York: Columbia University Press, 2015) p. 51.
17 Drucker, J. "Graphic Devices: Narration and Navigation" *Narrative* vol. 16, no. 2. (May, 2008) pp. 121–125.
18 Drucker, J. "Graphic Devices: Narration and Navigation" *Narrative* vol. 16, no. 2. (May, 2008) pp. 121–125.
19 Eco, U. *A Theory of Semiotics* (Bloomington: Indiana University Press, 1979) pp. 137–138.
20 von Arx, P. *Film Design* (Bern; Stuttgart: Haupt, 1983).
21 Woolman, M. and Bellantoni, J. *Moving Type: Designing for Time and Space* (East Sussex: RotoVision, 2000) p. 17.
22 Lupton, E. and Miller, A. *Design Writing Research: Writing on Graphic Design* (New York: Phaidon, 1996) p. 14.
23 Leborg, C. *Visual Grammar* (New York: Princeton Architectural Press, 2006) pp. 48–49.
24 Weibel, P. "Preface" *Typemotion* ed. Bernd Scheffer, Christine Stenzer, Peter Weibel and Soenke Zehle (Karlsruhe: Hatje Cantz/ZKM, 2015) pp. 8–11.
25 McLuhan, M. *The Gutenberg Galaxy: The Making of Typographic Man* (Toronto: University of Toronto Press, 1962).
26 McLuhan, M. *The Gutenberg Galaxy: The Making of Typographic Man* (Toronto: University of Toronto Press, 1962) p. 184.
27 Eisenstein, E. *The Printing Press as an Agent of Change* (Cambridge: Cambridge University Press: 1980).
28 Bühler, C. *The Fifteenth Century Book: the Scribes, the Printers, the Decorators* (Philadelphia: University of Pennsylvania Press, 1960) pp. 24–28.
29 Tschichold, J. *The New Typography* trans. Ruari McLean (Berkeley: University of California Press, 1998).
30 Warde, B. *The Crystal Goblet, Sixteen Essays on Typography* (London: Sylvan Press, 1955).
31 Greenberg, C. "Modernist Painting" *Clement Greenberg: The Collected Essays and Criticism, Volume 4* ed. John O'Brian (Chicago: University of Chicago Press, 1993) p. 86.
32 Helfand, J. *Screen: Essays on Graphic Design, New Media, and Visual Culture* (Princeton: Princeton Architectural Press, 2001) pp. 105–110.
33 Betancourt, M. "Experimental Animation and Motion Graphics" *Experimental Animation: From Analogue to Digital* ed. Miriam Harris, Lilly Husbands and Paul Taberham (New York: Routledge, 2018).
34 Spigel, L. *TV by Design: Modern Art and the Rise of Network Television* (Chicago: University of Chicago Press, 2008).
35 Dawson, M. "Edward Wesson and Merle Armitage" *LA's Early Moderns: Art, Architecture, Photography* ed. Victoria Dailey, Natalie Shivers and Michael Dawson (Los Angeles: Balcony Press, 2003) pp. 253–257.
36 Armitage, M. "Movie Titles" *Print* vol. 5, no. 2. (February 1, 1947) p. 45.
37 Golden, W. *The Visual Craft of William Golden* (New York: George Braziller, 1962) p. 21.

38 The double colon /::/ designates positions of mutual exclusion that define the scope of a dynamic range, which includes hybrid intermediaries and exhibits a contingent, metastable flux within that range.
39 McCoy, K. "American Graphic design Expression" *Design Quarterly* no. 148 (1990) pp. 4–22.
40 Aldersey-Williams, H. *The New Cranbrook Design Discourse* (New York: Rizzoli, 1990).
41 Bachfischer, G. and Robertson, T. "From Movable Type to Moving Type—Evolution in Technological Mediated Typography" (paper presented at the *Apple University Consortium Conference*, 2005) p. 9.
42 Lupton, E. "The Academy of Deconstructed Design" *Eye* vol. 1, no. 3. (Winter 1991) pp. 44–52.
43 Brownie, B. *Transforming Type: New Directions in Motion Typography* (New York: Bloomsbury, 2015) p. 15.
44 Betancourt, M. "Disruptive Technology: The Avant–Gardness of Avant–Garde Art" Article: a107, *CTheory* (May 1, 2002).
45 Stiegler, B. *Technics and Time 1: The Fault of Epimetheus* (Stanford: Stanford University Press, 1998) p. 77.
46 Stiegler, B. "Anamnesis and Hypomnesis: The Memories of Desire" *Technics* ed. Arthur Bradley and Louis Armand (Prague: Litteraria Pragensia, 2006) pp. 15–41.
47 Stiegler, B. *Technics and Time 3: Cinematic Time and the Question of Malaise* (Stanford: Stanford University Press, 2011) pp. 37–40.
48 Stiegler, B. *Technics and Time 3: Cinematic Time and the Question of Malaise* (Stanford: Stanford University Press, 2011) p. 19.
49 Hagener, M., Hediger V. and Strohmaier, A. *The State of Post-Cinema* (London: Palgrave, 2016) p. 3.
50 Shaviro, S. *Post Cinematic Affect* (Washington: Zero Books, 2010) p. 2.
51 Berry, D. and Dieter, M. "Thinking Postdigital Aesthetics: Art, Computation, Design" *The State of Post-Cinema* ed. Berry, D. and Dieter, M. (New York: Palgrave Macmillan, 2015) pp. 2–3.
52 Gaudreault, A. and Marion, P. *Kinematic Turn: Film in the Digital Era and Its Ten Problems* trans. Timothy Barnard (Montreal: Caboose Books, 2012) p. 40.
53 Gaudreault, A. and Marion, P. *Kinematic Turn: Film in the Digital Era and Its Ten Problems* trans. Timothy Barnard (Montreal: Caboose Books, 2012) p. 39.
54 Betancourt, M. *The History of Motion Graphics: From Avant-Garde to Industry in the United States* (Holicong: Wildside Press, 2013).
55 Fielding, R. *A Technological History of Motion Pictures and Television* (Berkeley: University of California Press, 1967) np.
56 Vogel, A. *Film as a Subversive Art* (New York: D.A.P., 1974).
57 Fielding, R. *The Technique of Special Effects Cinematography* (New York: Focal Press, 1984) pp. 405–406.
58 Manovich, L. "Understanding Meta-Media" *CTheory* (October 26, 2005).
59 Betancourt, M. "Experimental Animation and Motion Graphics" *Experimental Animation: From Analogue to Digital* ed. Miriam Harris, Lilly Husbands and Paul Taberham (New York: Routledge, 2018).

60 Betancourt, M. *The History of Motion Graphics: From Avant-Garde to Industry in the United States* (Holicong: Wildside Press, 2013) pp. 32–34.
61 Seldes, G. “Some Amateur Movies” *The New Republic* (March 6, 1929). pp. 71–72.
62 Leonard, H. *The Film Index: Volume 1 The Film as Art* (Arno Press, 1966) p. xxix.
63 Metz, C. *Impersonal Enunciation, or the Place of Film* trans. Corman Deane (New York: Columbia University Press, 2015) pp. 46–51.
64 Leonard, H. *The Film Index: Volume 1 The Film as Art* (Arno Press, 1966) p. xxix.
65 Bardèche, M. and Brasillach, R. *The History of Motion Pictures* trans. Isis Barry (New York: Norton, 1938) pp. 238.
66 Foucault, M. *This is not a Pipe* (Berkeley: University of California Press, 1982) p. 21.
67 Chisholm, B. “Reading Intertitles” *Journal of Popular Film and Television* vol. 15, no. 3. (1988) pp. 137–142.
68 Eco, U. “Interpreting Serials” *The Limits of Interpretation* (Bloomington: University of Indiana Press, 1994) pp. 86–87.
69 Eco, U. “Interpreting Serials” *The Limits of Interpretation* (Bloomington: University of Indiana Press, 1994) pp. 91–93.
70 Eco, U. “Interpreting Serials” *The Limits of Interpretation* (Bloomington: University of Indiana Press, 1994) pp. 88–99.
71 Metz, C. *Impersonal Enunciation, or the Place of Film* trans. Corman Deane (New York: Columbia University Press, 2015) pp. 46–51.
72 Drucker, J. “Graphic Devices: Narration and Navigation” *Narrative* vol. 16, no. 2. (May 2008) p. 121.
73 Betancourt, M. *The History of Motion Graphics: From Avant-Garde to Industry in the United States* (Holicong: Wildside Press, 2013). pp. 32–34.

THE 'READING-IMAGE'

The three modes of 'reading-image' depend on audience recognitions of visual form and lexical form as equally significant to interpretation:

1. a *kinetic action* encompasses discrete movements independent of the overall *kinesis* of the typography
2. a *graphic expression* employs visual forms that shift in role between *being-image* and *being-typography*
3. a *chronic progression* refers to the emergence of meaning across the design as a whole, a function of its duration and the complete series of movements and actions shown on-screen

Motion graphics expands the *implicit* time of lexical recognition into a *literal* duration, which the 'reading-image' demonstrates as the essential difference between motion and static typography. These modulations enable a playing-out on-screen of the interpretive process, externalizing what in static designs are internal recognitions as the visuality and presentation of the motion typography itself. The delay of lexical recognition versus immanent encounter becomes an oppositional activity that 'externalizes' the thought process of *reading* as/in the appearance-presentation of the text. These identifications define motion graphics via *kinesis* as fundamentally unlike graphic design.

1 Kinetic Action

Typography occupies an obvious overlap between the established and well-theorized field of graphic design and the newer, under-theorized field of motion graphics. The relevance and relationship of the formal models of graphic design for motion pictures are a topic of theoretical and critical dispute, with some historians and theorists of motion graphics arguing for a continuity and applicability of the conventions of static typography to the animated designs of motion pictures.[1] Differences between moving typography and static typography are typically masked by discussions that confuse formal issues of visuality::legibility with theory. These engagements begin by assuming the fundamental similarity of motion and static design—especially that typography remains constant, always determined, establishing a fixed role in semiosis—leading to the fallacy that motion graphics is a fusion of graphic design with the techniques of movement developed in animation; denying the relevance of cinema semiotics for motion graphics accompanies this category error.

Although animated logos, information graphics, and other types of moving design have been an aspect of motion pictures almost since their inception in the 1890s, their production and complexity have changed over time as new technologies that are cheaper, more efficient, and offer greater precision became standard practices. These changes enabled the increased complexity evident in the progression from early motion pictures that emphasized hand-animation to contemporary digital software that automates many of the most repetitious parts of the production process and allows a dynamic integration of animation with photography. This technical shift has been especially revolutionary for motion typography, enabling it to become commonplace and nearly invisible. However, this digital revolution has only impacted the means of production, leaving the foundational morphology and structure of their historical origins in animation intact. The addition of motion (and thus of organized time) to the otherwise immanent and static constructions of graphic design is basically transformative. The change from *immanence* (static design) to *emergence* (motion design) requires the same dynamic planning and orchestration common to cinema generally—in both animation and live action—situating motion graphics as an intermediary between them, incorporating both types of moving image. Equating the organization and theorization of all *motion* typography with the *static* typography of graphic design thus reflects a category error.

Viewers organize their perceptions by assigning category membership: positioned *before* any particular statement or meaning, category assignment[2] establishes all engagements within ranges of potential *prior* to their higher-level signification. These identifications typically happen autonomously, allowing the process of reading text, the dynamic of visuality::legibility, to occur almost instantaneously: *perception* is contingent, but at the same time entangled with cultural knowledge learned and gained through past experiences. The 'reading-image' is a modulated delay in this identification, its spacing-out as a series of visual and non-lexical identities, each articulated in itself, rather than as a singular, direct recognition that *reads* the text. This modal shift considers visual form as significance; however, even transforming *seeing* into *reading* requires training, a learned process, limited by fluency in the particular language itself. The fleeting perceptual encounter identified by Michel Foucault's 'enunciative function' describes the recognition of form and imagery in the arrangement of 'signs'—language—enabling audiences to understand a particular and 'precise' application of their internalized knowledge (the dynamic of visuality::legibility). Encultured protocols for semiosis and the grammatical order thus create the possibility for meaning:

> The statement is neither a syntagma, nor a rule of construction, nor a canonic form of succession and permutation; it is that which enables such groups of signs to exist, and enables these rules or forms to become manifest. But although it enables them to exist, it does so in a special way—a way that must not be confused with the existence of signs as elements of a language (*langue*), or with the material existence of those marks that occupy a fragment of space or last for a variable length of time.[3]

Foucault's semiotic hierarchy of *reading–seeing–hearing* enables an 'aura of textuality' to envelop the visual, apparent in the recognition of text, informing and overriding its visuality in the same way that semiosis elides the letterforms as they are subsumed into words and interpreted as the meaning conveyed. To assign the category of 'language' to any encounter is to presume an intentional purpose, that it communicates something, even or especially when that meaning remains unknown. Any freedom from imposed orders must be actively created for static texts, a choice not to follow the trained progression into signification; in motion typography this change from visuality to legibility *can* become an element of its presentation on-screen, a rendering of lexical engagement as immanent encounter. Semiosis for typography in *motion* accentuates rather than denies the dynamic of visuality::legibility, adding entirely novel dimensions of a literally *temporal* emergence, development, and recognition to what is already a complex interplay of perception and lexical expertise. The identification of language—type—that is *reading* depends on a particular engagement guided by the audience's familiarity with written languages, a distinct and parallel mode of engagement from their visual perceptions. The textual encounter is independent of any imagery appearing alongside the text, and requires the letterforms to assume an identity apart from graphic marks—a becoming-words that is the linguistic. In contradistinction to how motion graphics overlap with some of the concerns established in graphic design's use of typography, their superficial relationship to established methodologies for static design does not alter the essential difference that movement on-screen and development over time makes for lexical recognition. Movement entails a *becoming*.

Complicating visuality::legibility are theories of *motion* as an expressive part of narrative cinema that are commonly and logically focused on the dynamics of the *shot*. This concern is foundational to Giles Deleuze's analysis of the 'movement-image' in *Cinema 1*, but offers a theorization explicitly and only concerned with the arrangement and development of narrative fictions—any consideration of graphic, animated, or moving elements beyond these strictures is outside the scope of his analysis, yet the discussion of *kinetics* converges on his concerns with the expressivity of movement; the differences lie with *what* is being expressed. The mismatch between Deleuze's theory and the composed, precisely determinate, and controlled actions of the animated film is an immediate feature of his 'movement' in the autonomous *recording* of kinematography:

> The image of the cinema being, therefore, 'automatic' and presented primarily as *movement-image*, we have considered under what conditions it is specifically defined into different types. These types are, principally, the *perception-image*, the *affection-image* and the *action-image*. Their distribution certainly does determine a representation of time, but it must be noted that time remains the object of an indirect representation in so far as it depends on montage and derives from movement-images.[4]

Animation does not 'fit' this elemental description of motion: it is constructed, a fabricated invention composed by manipulating the interpreted *changes* created inbetween the frames shown on-screen: the suggestion of its being a material trace of the apparent reality shown on-screen is simply ridiculous; with digitally generated elements this indexicality, however tenuous, vanishes. The higher-level decomposition of 'movement-image' into subtypes retains the imprint of this initial capturing of an autonomous reality. The typology that Deleuze offers specifically cannot describe the animated film, and thus cannot describe the *kinesis* of typographic motion with his 'movement-image.' The unity of the shot that allows its fragmentation makes an interpretation of the world shown. The types of 'movement-image' Deleuze identifies are fundamentally and irreducibly narrative: instances of a presented 'perception' connected to a character (dream, hallucination, subjective view), 'affection' (the visible space as an arena for/awaiting action), or 'action' (the continuity of cause–effect within/across a series of shots). They rely on the premise of a world-on-film that corresponds to the parameters of experiential reality and whose causality continues to apply in cinema. This basis is a contingency in animation, which unlike the live action motion picture must not automatically correspond to the assumptions of reality, nor does its presence on-screen extend beyond the parameters of its appearance in the shot. It is not appropriate to talk about *animated* events not 'captured' by the camera, what happened before the shot, or after its conclusion. In the artificial construction of the animated film, there is no before or after, only what appears on-screen—shots whose contents are plastic and contingent—contradicting the conception of *dureé* taken from Henri Bergson's philosophy that is the exploratory premise of Deleuze's proposal. The observational basis of the 'movement-image' lies with its encoding as a trace of lived changes seen in the world and held for analysis/consideration in/as the narrative constructions familiar from fiction films, thereby enabling their comprehension through the justifications of narration and *fabula*. Distinguishing the 'reading-image' reveals inherent differences arising in the role of narrative for Deleuze's typology and its connection to the indexicality of photography, giving the 'reading-image' a general relevance for digital cinema, animation, motion graphics, and VFX.

The precession of images within the 'movement-image' all depend on the extractive nature of live action kinematography employed for narrative (if not fictive) purposes. The 'perception-image' is a narrative construction of *how* the shot fits within the *fabula*; it is an explanation/justification of what appears as an *objective* presentation (that identifies impressions, hallucinations, dreams within the narrative progression), as a *subjective* elaboration of character consciousness (changes of duration, a demonstration of character point-of-view), or as a material revelation of the whole (as with speed ramping, slow or fast motion, hold frames) that manipulates the shot as a structural unit. These propositions are an identification of *narrative functions*, dependent upon audience interpretations for their comprehension and realization—they are not identifications of the visuality or motion of the shot, but of the role it plays in the enunciation of *fabula* and its relationship to the diegesis. These restrictions and foundational roles separate the 'movement-image' from its apparent relevance for the analysis of animation. Even though the subtypes Deleuze proposes, 'affection-image' and 'action-image,' suggest a descriptive utility for identifying the movements of animated graphics, their comprehension depends on the 'motive' proposed by the *narrative function* created in the initial 'perception-image' and its justification for the actions shown through recourse to fictive drama.

The phenomenological basis of this analytic in the narrative context and the identification of the 'movement-image' arises in the equation of *cinema=narrative*, a relationship that requires an indexical link of photography to 'the real' for its coherence (as 'cinematic realism'), implicitly offered by his selections from the "great films" for analysis—feature-length productions such as Dreyer's *The Passion of Joan of Arc* or Chaplin's films. Deleuze constructs *cinema=narrative* with a teleological organization: his focus on 'classical cinema' (the "great films") means that established, familiar norms from narrative cinema limit his analysis. The "Preface to the French edition" at the start of *Cinema 1: The Movement-Image* makes these restrictions obvious without articulating what they mean for the elision of alternatives:

> In this first part we will deal with the movement-image and its varieties. The time-image will be the subject of a second part. The great directors of cinema may be compared, in our view, not merely with painters, architects and musicians, but also with thinkers. They think with movement-images and time-images instead of concepts.[5]

Teleology takes the applications by the "great directors of cinema" as the whole and entirety of cinematic application, constructing an argument around their narrative, dramatic, feature-length productions that affirms their selection, but produces a framework that does not extend beyond them. The use of story-based justifications for audience interpretations cannot really describe what happens with the lexicality of motion typography offering *non-narrative* expressions formed by *kinesis* divorced from realist storytelling. This textual dimension receives neither consideration nor discussion in Deleuze's analysis precisely because the 'reading-image' offers a moment of engagement where semiotic recognition removes typo/graphics (completely or at least partially) from the realm of realist pictorialism, thus beyond the scope of his analysis. Deleuze's concerns lie exclusively with the constructions of narrative, realist fictions; their even application to documentary is problematic. His consideration of the fictive world-on-film concerns how that world comes into being through images. This theory superficially resembles the realist understandings of cinema offered by Stanley Cavell and André Bazin—Deleuze's approach, however, differs. It takes the 'reality' on film as a given *construct*, produced and maintained not through an ontological connection to a pro-filmic reality, but phenomenologically as a modeling of characters and narration-experiences *in* the presentation (but which still retains the indexicality of photography). His analysis attempts to resolve the hermetic disconnection between semiotics, narrative, and motion pictures that he identifies in *Cinema 2*:

> The principle according to which linguistics is only a part of semiology is thus realized in the definition of languages without a language system (*semes*), which includes the cinema as well as the languages of gestures, clothing or music. There is therefore no reason to look for features in cinema that only belong to a language system, like double articulation. On the other hand, language features which necessarily apply to utterances will be found in the cinema, as rules of use, in the language system and outside of it: the syntagm (conjunction of present relative units) and the paradigm (disjunction of present units with comparable absent units). The semiology of cinema will be the discipline that applies linguistic models, especially syntagmatic ones, to images as constituting one of their principal 'codes.' We are moving in a strange circle here, because syntagmatics assumes that the image can be assimilated to an utterance, but it is also what makes the image by right assimilable to the utterance. It is a typically Kantian vicious circle: syntagmatics applies because the image is an utterance, but the image is an utterance because it is subject to syntagmatics.[6]

Deleuze's analysis attempts to escape the circularity of semiotics for the 'non-linguistic statements' of pure visual articulation, a discrepancy that arises precisely because these dynamics are lexical without familiar determinate signifieds. The expressiveness of *kinetic actions* arises in their interruption of this semiotic recognition to bring the visual *back* into analysis and consideration, but without the attendant circularity and paradox Deleuze identifies. The paradox he notes is resolved in the conception of this semiotic approach as only one potential within a range whose validity is not provided by their descriptive/explanatory potential, but by their membership within the range itself. The validity of the set as a whole replaces the circular justification with a state of information where one interpretation (or paradigm) is justified by its inclusion within a field of other potentials, each of which validates the others—the state of information presents a multiplicity and continuity that denies the logical sequence (it is *alinear* rather than *non-linear*), thus avoiding circularity. Viewing interpretation as ranges of equally valid yet incompatible sets of potential probabilities means abandoning singular, absolute results, thus enabling the dynamics of interpretation revealed by the 'reading-image' and its instability of visuality::legibility. This foundation opens the range of potential interpretations without sacrificing validity or truth, which then become additional dimensions within a multidimensional nodal 'space.'[7] Reading is a distinct action from seeing, one that transforms graphics into typography, a dominant mode where the image becomes an irrelevant dimension to the legibility and lexicality of the text-being-seen after its identification *qua* text. These obvious features of the static textual work become dynamic, even optional for motion typography, revealing the role of the 'reading-image' in distinguishing between motion and static typography. The *kinetic action*, *graphic expression*, and *chronic progression* modes offer semiotic registers that expand the range of structural and immanent features of lexicality contained in the arrangements of typefaces, page sizes, headers, footers, and columns common to graphic design. However, purely *kinetic actions* are rare; more common are *graphic expressions* and *chronic progression*.

The title sequence for *Psycho* (1960), designed by Saul Bass, is typical of the Early Phase of the Designer Period,[8] which adapted Modernist approaches to graphic design into the organization and animation of motion graphics [Figure 1.1].[9] Its recreation in color by Pablo Ferro for Gus Van Sant's 1998 remake retained the same dynamics of animated lines, adding color, but not changing the *kinetic actions* in Bass's original design. The animated type in the main title card presents shifting/dividing letterforms as performances of discrete movements. Animations articulate the 'reading-image' in movements performed *by* the word "PSYCHO" as discrete units, revealing a hierarchy of durations: the immanent proximity of the events shown (*kinetic action*), and the higher-level order of their place with the development of the whole (*chronic progression*). The splitting and shifting text in *Psycho* enters and exits with a different valence than once it takes shape. The repeating coming-together and breaking-apart of this typography can be understood as a conventional transition, perhaps itself significant, but equally dismissible as *not* signifying. The small, shifting motions once the word "PSYCHO" has taken shape—its *kinetic actions*—contrast with how the letterforms enter and exit the screen, invoking an understanding of their *kinesis* as intentional, inviting their consideration as more than just decorative or transitional. This realization creates the 'reading-image.' The

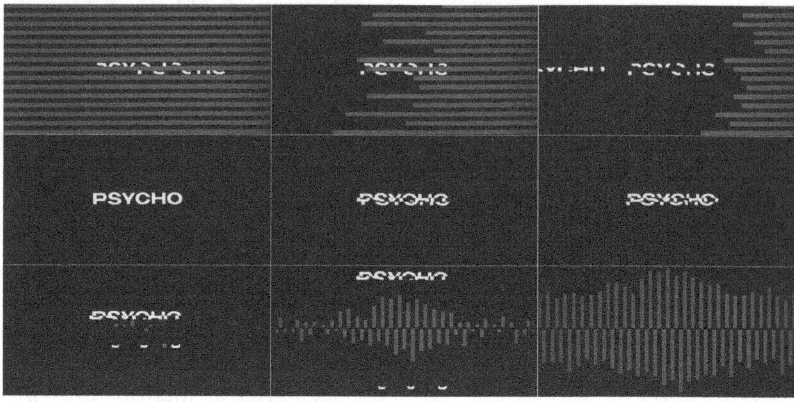

Figure 1.1 Stills showing the animated entrance [Top], kinetic motions [Middle], and exit [Bottom] of the main title card for *Psycho* (1960), designed by Saul Bass

recognition of the actions in the main title card leads to a consideration of the transitions: if one set of divisions is significant, the others may be as well; recognizing *all* the splits *as* meaningful only happens because the momentary re/splitting *kinetic action* that divides the letters in the "PSYCHO" title card justifies (or maybe *demands*) a reconsideration of the other transition-splits as being *more* than merely transitional (i.e. as a *chronic progression*).

The morphology of the actions is simple, constant; however, their *meaningful* structure depends on the audience interpreting them through a dynamics based in an indirect narrative linkage and intratextual dialogue. The words' fragmented and unstable shape becomes meaningful even when these internal textual divisions are invisible as an expression of (hidden) psychosis. Allegorical connections between design and story are typical of Bass's conception of the title sequence as a reiteration of the drama, which he explains in a discussion with film historian Pamela Haskin:

> My initial thoughts about what a title could do was to set mood and to prime the underlying core of the film's story; to express the story in some metaphorical way. I saw the title as a way of conditioning the audience, so that when the film actually began, viewers would already have an emotional resonance with it.[10]

The concern Bass describes with the "underlying core of the film's story" demands an allegorical mode of engagement for its relationship to the narrative to become apparent. This suggestion apparently invokes Deleuze's 'movement-image' without employing it: the symbolic content of the *Psycho* sequence, apart from its lexical significance as a collection and listing of names and production roles, is indexical—an emergent recognition that depends on its lexicality to create *narrative function*. The relationship between this animation, the film title "PSYCHO," and schizophrenia is readily apparent on reflection, if not immanent in the text; the medical term "schizophrenia" is a conjunction of Greek and Latin elements that individually mean "splitting" and "mind." The disease is characterized by a mental breaking-apart that Bass dramatized as the *literal* fragmentation of the letterforms—visible as their *kinetic actions*. Interpreting the movements in the word "PSYCHO" depends on exactly this splitting, metonymous with the events of the narrative, enabling the audience to anticipate what will happen in the film that follows *if* they are aware of the story. Shifts in audience engagement from reading to allegory, a 'symbolic dimension,' are typical of the concerns with 'symbology' by graphic designers in the 1950s and 1960s: the aspiration and attempt to create universally comprehensible graphics and imagery that signify without the formal encoding typical of written or spoken languages.[11] The kinetic offers an excess of signification, separate from that of the lexical presentation; this approach renders the typo/graphics performative (their formal motions become signifiers), much like an actor's gestures or the conventionalized postures and expressions of theatrical traditions such as the *Commedia dell'Arte*[12] and Japanese *Kabuki* theater,[13] where stylized actions serve precisely understood emotive and lexical ends, but which are *not* themselves lexical. The complex web of past experience and established knowledge required for these traditional metalinguistic performances are specific products of encultured expertise; for Modernist designs, this already known dimension finds analogous supports through the contextual role of the expressions in relation to the self-definitions produced through the rest of the work; for *Psycho*, the narrative about Norman Bates's murderous psychosis provides the hidden (allegorical) signified.

The expressiveness of the dis/continuous motion employed in *Psycho* informs the *contrast* that identifies which movements are (potentially) significant expressions. However, this recognition is not only an *intra*textual marking between one element and another; the anticipated *inter*textual order also determines expectations that are essential to distinguishing significant from insignificant. Scrolling text is a common, standard part of film titles, a listing of the production that moves at a steady, continuous pace in openings such as *Chinatown* (1974), designed by Wayne Fitzgerald; in the uncredited titles for *The Shining* (1980); or the credits that scroll in reverse order, gradually deregistering to move sideways off-screen, in director Gaspar Noé's *Irréversible* (2002). These continuously moving texts do not normally invite a consideration of their *kinesis* as significant. The organization of title cards/background photography in *The Shining* serves to isolate the individual credits, but does not eliminate the sense of their motion as a unitary progression where the text and image proceed as separate, distinct elements (the figure–ground mode).[14] Scrolling texts do not normally express an important aspect of the lexical meaning, performing instead an articulative role, breaking the text into parts. In Richard Serra and Carlotta Fay Schoolman's videotape *Television Delivers People* (1973), made with simple white text on a blue background that moves vertically up the screen, the gaps and 'pauses' between texts in this presentation serve to organize the text for ease of reading and separate it into three sections, much like the breaking-up of paragraphs and pages of printed text. These articulations do not alter the contents or meaning of the text, but do improve its legibility—just as the spacing and edits of scrolling text in the second part of Dara Birnbaum's remix videotape *Technology Transformation: Wonder Woman* (1978) synchronize the words on-screen with the sung lyrics, making the contents of the song a point of explicit awareness. The scrolling text as such only becomes apparent in Birnbaum's tape when the edits happen in the middle of its ascent up the screen: the sudden change acts like a 'jump cut' in the continuity of motion, but this rupture draws attention to the synchronization of text to lyrics—the literalization of the audible in the visible text—rather than to the artifice created in/by the motion. Similar synchronizations of lyrics sung with words on-screen are a commonality of music videos. The integration of lyrics with imagery in the design by Corinne Bance and Axel d'Harcourt for the 2010 music video to *Symphonies (title sequences)* by Dan Black dynamically shifts and rearranges text–image composites to explicitly evoke feature film title sequences. All of these examples employ motion typography for fundamentally the same 'transparent' presentation, familiar and learned through intertextual experience in reading lexical content, rather than as a component of expressive modulation. This invisibility is normal; expressivity is the exception.

The differences between these typical approaches to scrolling text and the content provided by its kinetic expressions posed in Canadian animator Marv Newland's two-minute animated film composed from an animated fawn and a collection of scrolling credits, *Bambi Meets Godzilla* (1969) [Figure 1.2], depends on the intratextual distinctions between the different title cards as they scroll up the screen, coupled with how they violate intertextual expectations. The inconsistency of the animation *for* each title card while it scrolls up the screen, coupled with the constantly shifting roles for Marv Newland in the production (he is credited for almost every role in the film), draws attention to the

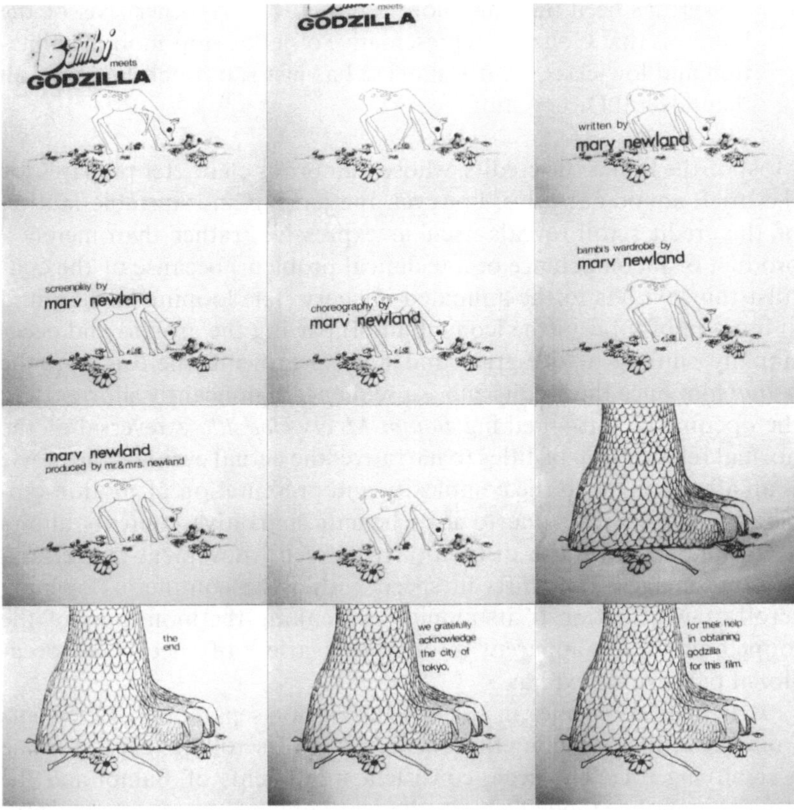

Figure 1.2 Stills from *Bambi Meets Godzilla* (1969) by Marv Newland

conventional nature of this presentation, reinforcing its parodic character.[15] In *Bambi Meets Godzilla* the scrolling text has an unsteady progression up the screen, offering a critique of familiar, Disney animation, as film critic Jami Bernard explains in *The Fifty Greatest Cartoons as Selected by 1,000 Animation Professionals*:

> The gentle, reassuring music and pronounced lack of action established Bambi as an icon rather than a character, not just a cute deer in the forest, but the archetypal Disney creation with all the emotional baggage that comes with it—family values, children's entertainment, good taste, the middle class order. Then—serenity interruptus. The quick stomping on the deer by Godzilla—the pacing of the cartoon up to and including the credits is masterful—is funny on several levels. One is that the title of the cartoon did not

> tip us off to the nature of the punch line, as it should have if the viewer has been thinking more carefully. [...] Another level of the humor is that Godzilla, representative of jerky, stop-motion animation and low-class, sci-fi B movies, has just run roughshod over all that tasteful Disney stuff.[16]

Most of the film is the credits, whose humorous character prepares for the brief, comic narrative; however, the jerking and unstable motion of the credit scroll reveals itself as expressive (rather than merely a product of incompetence or a technical problem) because of the contrast this text has to the animated imagery. The looping background animation of a fawn (the iconic Bambi) pawing the ground and occasionally sniffing at the grass and flowers growing there is also the *actual* film once the credits end—a sequence significantly shorter than the opening credits—making *Bambi Meets Godzilla* a reversal of the normal relationship of titles to narrative: the actual event of the movie is an afterthought to the complexity and presentation of motion typography. This work, due to its schematic narrative contents allows a consideration of the distinctions between 'movement-image' and 'reading-image.' The shifts in speed within the continuous opening scroll draw attention to its animation, making the monotony of the looped animation apparent through the variety of speeds and occasional pauses the text has.

Articulation emerges in the spacing-out or separation of elements from each other, enabling the *kinetic action* of scrolling text to assume a signifying role. The even, consistent movements of Bambi and the equally immobile Godzilla make the scroll obvious as an *animated* process. This text is more than just a series of letters and words—it is a parody of titling, a fact reiterated by the choices of the credits themselves, each of which moves with its own, particular character, giving each title card its own *kinetic action*. These distinctions from the background animation make the 'reading-image' apparent. Understanding the humor requires the interaction between its animated motion (visuality) and the lexicality. Because each title card moves in its own way, with distinctive shifts in speed, alignment, and progress up the screen, each credit offers a unique expression that draws attention to the smooth and 'invisible' motion normally expected, as well as the seamless looping actions of Bambi (Deleuze's 'movement-image' that lies behind these texts). This intertextual recognition of what is expected, doubled by the individual differences in/between each card, differentiates the *kinetic action* of single motions from the *chronic progression* of the whole design: they remain singular instances, each progressing in a unique, independent way that is entirely different from all the others. Their interaction with the realist imagery in the background defines them as a discrete 'moment' within the work, the 'reading-image,' parallel and dominant over the pictorial background in a reminder of Foucault's *reading–seeing–hearing* hierarchy.

As *Bambi Meets Godzilla* shows, *kinetic actions* are not necessarily signs of madness. Apprehending the actions in both *Bambi Meets Godzilla* and *Psycho* as self-contained expressions shifts their understanding so they are not merely stylized decorations—a moving analogue to the descenders, flourishes, and serifs of static typography—but a choice that depends on an autonomous decision by the audience to separate and engage a particular motion as an expressive action. The shifting and replacement of letters with numbers in Peter Frankfurt's title design for *The Number 23* (2007) [Figure 1.3] creates a very different expression from what Newland or Bass produced. The flickering dis/appearances suggests an instability of interpretation, while the short sequences invoke numerology by showing how groups of numbers always add up to 23 [Figure 1.4]. The uncanniness created by these repetitions rapidly develops into a presentation of paranoia, recalling Surrealist painter Salvador Dali's comments on the relationship between reality and delirium in his theorization of the 'paranoiac-critical method' for image composition:

> Paranoia uses the external world in order to assert its dominating idea and has the disturbing characteristic of making others accept this idea's reality. The reality of the external world is used for illustration and proof, and so comes to serve the reality of the mind.[17]

While Dali's concerns lie with the simulation of the synthetic and creative impacts of paranoia for Surrealist imagery, his theory is a closely argued consideration of schizophrenia and its mode of presentation. The conversion of facts into evidence that makes the paranoid fantasy seem credible is precisely the sum of the actions shown in *The Number 23*, a film whose protagonist, "Walter Sparrow" (played by Jim Carey), is gradually revealed to be living in a paranoid fugue state. As in *Psycho*, these animated texts are employed as a means to identify madness, an understandable conceit since the immobility of letters is an assurance of a stable order; for them to leap into motion, rearrange themselves, or turn into numbers is to throw that ordered reality into disarray.

The lexical order, as Michel Foucault's critique of the 'enunciative function' notes, is central to the stability of knowledge.[18] What *kinetic actions* performed by letterforms remind the viewer is that they have a configurable nature—that there are only a limited number of elements employed in all words. Their shifting positions become a symbolic

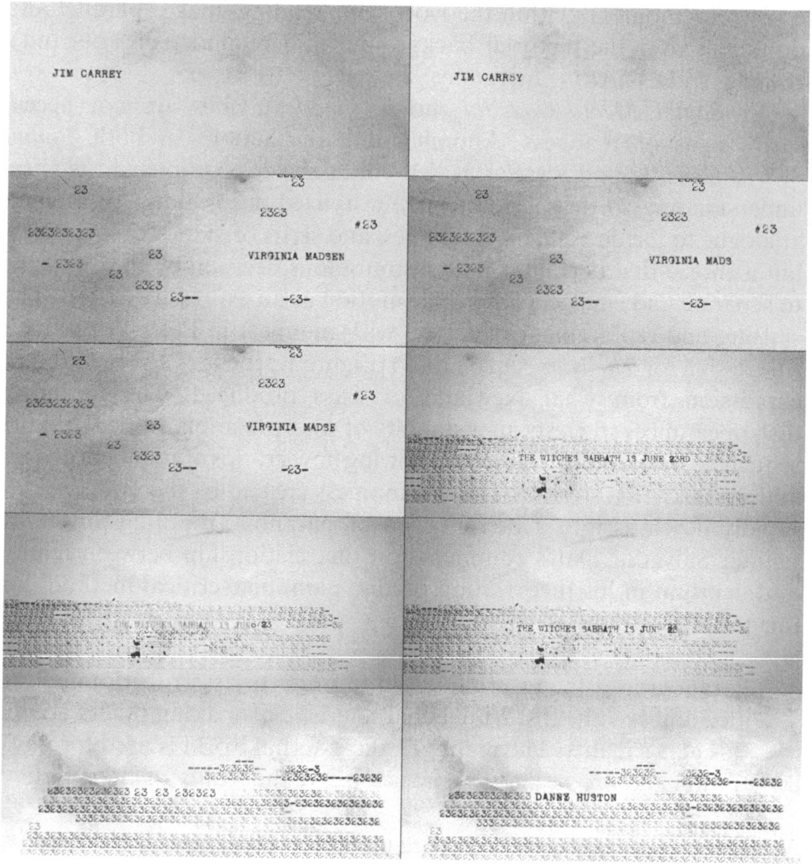

Figure 1.3 Selected stills from the title sequence for *The Number 23* (2007), designed by Peter Frankfurt, showing animation of text and substitution of numbers for letters

madness for the titles to *Psycho* and *The Number 23* precisely because, when the letters themselves are not merely animated but changing positions and identities within words, this movement also changes what the words themselves are. *Fluxfilm #29: Word Movie* (1966) is a silent animation by Paul Sharits that creates a singular series of shifting letter–word relations, undermining the unitary conception of language *as* text [Figure 1.5]. The pulsating text surrounding stable letters emphasizes their immobility apart from the words they form. The animation shifts attention from the words to the letters as independent entities in a fragmentation process that draws attention to the

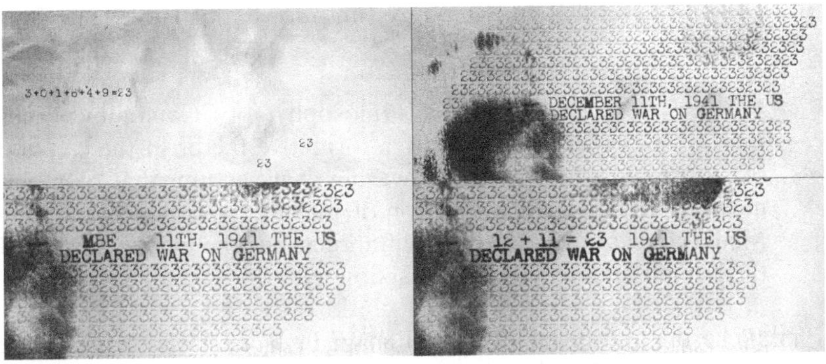

Figure 1.4 Examples of numerology from the title sequence for *The Number 23* (2007), designed by Peter Frankfurt

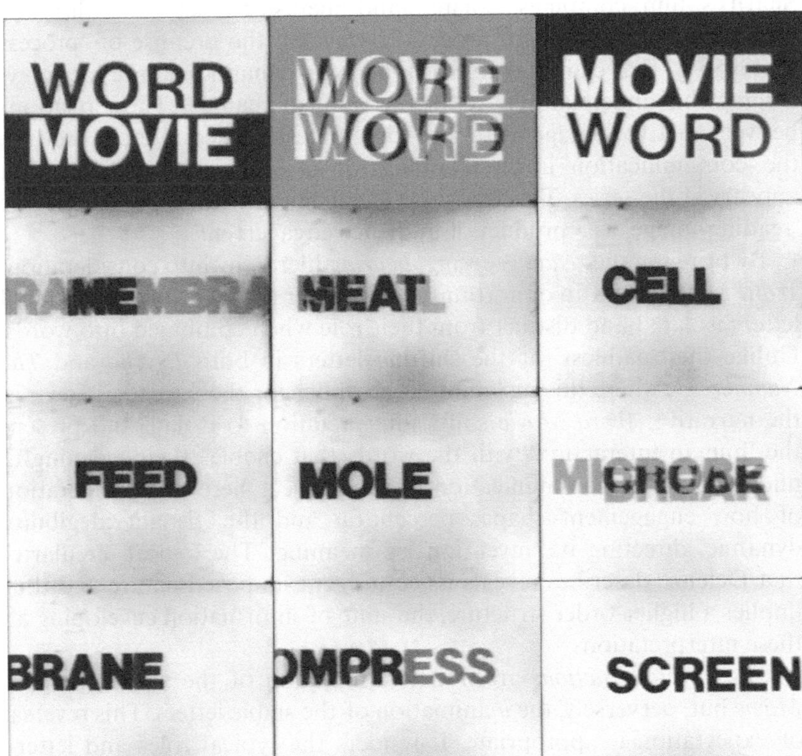

Figure 1.5 Stills from *Fluxfilm #29: Word Movie* (1966) by Paul Sharits

ordering role of the audience, as Sharits observes in a series of notes from 1965, "Several Premises on 'Assumptions' and How They Free the Writer":

> 4. (see "Process Oriented Philosophy of Communication," ETC): the reader is necessarily a formative factor in the creation of "meaning" when he reads anything (if we assume that "communication" is not the transmission of meaning) (see Understanding Media): meaning is not representational but the media itself (and the human interaction/or/transaction with the media.[19]

The flickering and instability of language in *Word Movie* brings these extracts from media theory into focus: they describe the *affective* dynamic between visuality::legibility where the words *read* are at the same time words *recognized*, identified, from the pulsating and semi-legible series of replacements and novel orderings flashing on-screen. Sharits's film combines isolated and metastable letters within the unstable configurations of words. To develop the premise of 'process philosophy' that claims ontological being is dynamic requires acknowledging this understanding in any account of reality.[20] These relations between active engagement and the material encountered produce the 'communication' in the identification of specific words from what appears in the series. This transitive engagement with words reveals the 'reading-image' as a product of audience engagement.

By bringing the *reading–seeing–hearing* hierarchy into consideration, *Word Movie* offers an opportunity to consider the identity of individual letters isolated and distinct from their role when combined into words. Unlike the 'madness' of the shifting letters in both *Psycho* and *The Number 23*, where this instability is a cypher for the psychosis sown in the narrative, *Word Movie* shifts interpretation to isolate and present the 'human interaction' with the words that enables their meaningful understanding. Communication is the subject here, a consideration of how engagement shapes perception and the visuality::legibility dynamic, directing its 'invention' of meaning. The logical circularity that Deleuze describes reveals its contingent, imposed nature and thus implies a higher-order structure, the state of information enveloping all these interpretations.

These *kinetic actions* are not the animation of the words in *Word Movie* but, perversely, the *in*animation of the stable letters. This reversal of expectation is appropriate. It renders the typical roles and letter–word relationships a self-conscious affect, imposed and created by the audience-who-reads. The 'reading-image' in *Word Movie* depicts the imposition of order in an inversion of Foucault's "empirical gaze," in which sight and vision become a metaphor for understanding:

> seeing consists in leaving to experience its greatest corporeal opacity; the solidity, the obscurity, the density of things closed in upon themselves, have powers of truth that they owe not to light, but to the slowness of the gaze that passes over them, around them, and gradually into them, bringing them nothing more than its own light. The residence of truth in the dark center of things is linked, paradoxically, to this sovereign power of *the empirical gaze* that turns their darkness into light.[21]

The words are created as the audience 'picks out' distinct arrangements from *Word Movie*: this imposed ordering is the subject of the film, rather than an immanent, affective process that happens invisibly. Watching Sharits's film requires an active engagement: parsing sensation into *significances* and *insignificances* is not an engagement with meaning or signification, but rather attracts, deflects, and organizes *attention*. It is a transfer of thinking into seeing, closing the letters in upon themselves in such a way that the audience cannot help but consider how reading speeds past their normal arrangements and even motion typography does not make their active role in articulating words necessarily apparent. The shifting breaks in *Psycho* and the swapping between letters and numbers in *The Number 23* do not affirm the role of letters, but the dominance of the established order that subsumes them.

In Norman McLaren's film *Blinkety Blank* (1955) the *kinetic action* does not suggest a changed consciousness; it is instead a movement synchronizing the typography with the rhythms of the soundtrack. Perception is absolute. The playful animation of the text offers a direct link to a static-like noise that pulsates on the soundtrack, each *pfff* sound happening simultaneously with the blinking movement of the credits [Figure 1.6]. This motion type parallels a similarly literal animation of the word "Itch" in *The Seven Year Itch* (1955), designed by Saul Bass, where the word 'scratches' itself. This direct connection of the animation to the title draws attention to each credit in turn. In McLaren's film the text blanks out, followed by a black frame. For example, the title card for the musicians comes after a series of other animated credits employing the same literal action and direct (illustrative) synchronization of image to sound. These connections naturalize the abstract link and peculiar affect of the words literally disappearing (blanking) for one frame, only to return in the next one. This motion repeats through the whole list of instruments and performers, each word synchronized, to disappear and then reappear in turn: the sounds signal the (absent, implied) movement. The relationship between sound and image is especially important for this film, apparent from the beginning with how the credits are linked to either the synthetic sounds of McLaren's drawn soundtrack or the musical cues provided by Blackburn's experimental

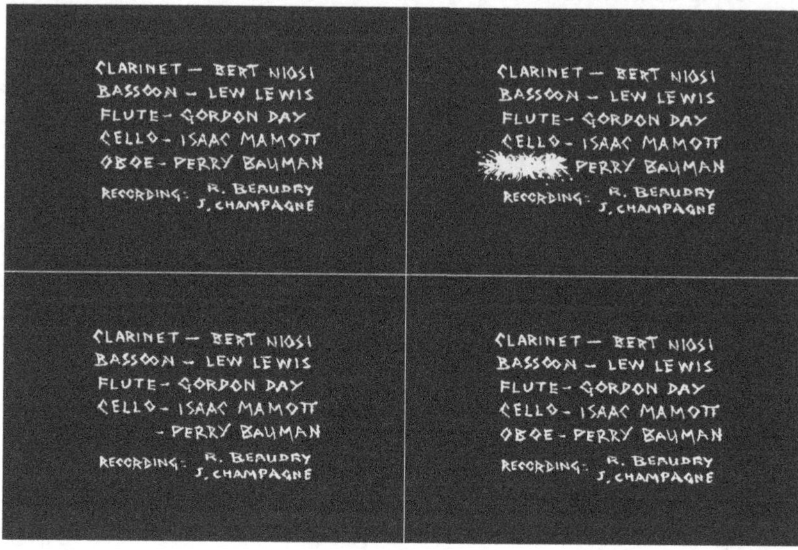

Figure 1.6 Four consecutive frames from the titles for *Blinkety Blank* (1955) by Norman McLaren, showing the word "OBOE" blink, disappear, and then return

score that reveals the impact of his studying aleoric composition in Paris during 1953: composed on a three-line stave without key signature, the performers were instructed to improvise pitch within a score focused on rhythm rather than tone.[22] This rhythmic basis matches the ambivalences of the animation, drawing attention to their expressive nature.

Without this initial foundation forming (in) the object perceived, the initial encounter does not become the *statement* that enables more familiar and elaborate networks of relationship, indexicality, and narrative in McLaren's film: dis/appearance characterizes the animation of two "birds" that interact in the film that follows, their motions following the same blink-then-blank progression shown in Figure 1.6, an illustration of the *literal* title of the film. The *kinesis* is strongly rhythmic, but without any *actual* animated motion. Although the title draws direct attention to this visual fact, the affect is entirely different, a reminder of McLaren's engagement with the animation process:

> The Philosophy Behind this Machine
> Animation is not the art of Drawings-that-move but the art of Movements-that-are-drawn.

> What happens between each frame is much more important than what exists on each frame.
>
> Animation is therefore the art of manipulating the invisible interstices that lie between frames.[23]

This syllogism precisely anticipates the manipulations appearing in *Blinkety Blank*. The perception of these words as rapidly 'popping' out of sight and returning a moment later arises as an explanation for what happened inbetween the individual frames—an action so swift that it was not captured on film. In proposing a cause-and-effect relationship, these animations converge on the explanations common to *narrative function*. These manipulations appear throughout the film, but are especially striking during the opening credits because text does not typically move in this way (or at all). It is a paradigmatic example of *kinetic action* ('reading-image'). The mental activity required to render this action coherent—as movement, as narrative—is an excess, entirely separate from the text, acknowledging the immanence of 'movement,' and the development of meaning 'contained' by the material object and technical apparatus depends on the mind of the audience.[24] Yet the animation of this apparent movement of blinks and blanks is linked not only to the behavior of that otherwise static text-on-screen, but to a reiteration of the film's title, drawing attention to it as a descriptive announcement of the animation process as a pun on a *censored* expletive: "blankety blank!" The duality of these meanings becomes apparent as the 'narrative' progresses; there is no coherent 'plot,' only a series of stream-of-consciousness activities in which a bird escapes its cage, plays dead, and interacts with another bird-being to eventually fuse into an egg that hatches—a Surrealistic progression in fragmentary, blinking animation synchronized to music by Maurice Blackburn. Recognizing this duality happens all at once or not at all, a realization guided by the *kinetic action* performed by the text anticipating the style of the animation that follows and matching the film title itself.

The 'reading-image' depends on this contingency of animation that exploits the innately sampled reality of motion pictures: the basic unit is not the 'shot' but the individual frame, where the on-screen imagery is always already subject to revision and plastic deformation. Audience perception renders the intermittent presentation of these stills as the continuous, dynamic 'reality' of movement; although the technology of digital imaging is vastly different from celluloid film or analogue video, the same experiential engagement creates movement for all three media. This technological basis instrumentalizes Ferdinand de Saussure's comment that "in language everything boils down to differences, but also to groupings."[25] The differences between frames beget movement; the grouping of frames into shots begets all the entangled higher-order interpretations of causality, narrative, and story. While interpretations in both motion pictures and lexical forms such as written or spoken languages *begin* with perception, for the semiotics of language, the audience's perceptions are not typically considered as an instrumentality of meaning; the 'reading-image' demonstrates they are for motion graphics, a reminder of its avant-garde heritage.[26] Thus each sequence of frames exists prior to the shot and its composition in/through montage: the frames determine (are) the nature of what appears on-screen and determine *if* it acts like an imaginary window offering a fictitious view into a world. The illusory, normative assumption that motion pictures are based in the shot gives the assumption of *cinema=narrative* a necessary and essential character. In contrast to this fallacy, evident in how Deleuze constructs the 'movement-image' and 'time-image,' the *apparent motion* of motion pictures should be understood as a mental process.[27] The movement we see when watching a movie—in any form, either as cinema, TV, or web video—is more than simply the illusion of motion; it is perceptually as *real* as any other perceived visual motion—there can be no separation of object seen from its interpretation. The experience of *sight* is a product of interpretations where past experiences inform the immediate sensory encounter, giving order to it by identifying what is and is not significant (requires attention). Thus, the 'reading-image' depends on earlier encounters with real, empirically immanent motion, distinguishing motion graphics from the metaphoric 'movement' of static graphic design.

The 'reading-image' offers the conscious engagement with the screen as a surface against narrative and realist considerations, offering instead a conception of the image as a domain of active participation and temporal activity, shifting throughout the hierarchy of *reading–seeing–hearing*, where the visual becomes subservient to the lexical. What Michel Foucault theorized as an actively engaged, organizational process determines denotation—it renders the empirical process of perception into 'markers' that give considerations of morphology and structure the superficial appearance of both a natural, unquestionable encounter, and transforms their analysis into a formalist rubric. Yet in being *potential*, these 'markers' are entirely subservient to the audience's internalized expectations and imposed coherence on what are continuous, inchoate, unstructured encounters. *Vision* for Foucault is coincident with a tendency towards a materialist understanding of the visible world, one where vision was equated with knowledge, and is specifically embodied in the "empirical gaze," an ideological use of sight/vision as metaphor for understanding.[28] This conception of vision is central to his critique of knowledge: in seeing the picture we do not read any accompanying text, but in reading that text the image necessarily becomes tangential to its informational contents. Enunciation mediates between the encounter in perception and its organization into the *statement*. For Foucault, vision provides more than just a metaphor for the organization of the world; it is an operative paradigm for comprehension, whether in a low-level recognition of form and imagery, or at a higher level, in the identification of *type*—language—that enables audiences to understand a particular and 'precise' application of their internalized, encultured protocols for semiosis and the grammatical order of *langue*. However, this transcendental, metaphysical comprehension (the cultural meaning of *sight* and *insight*) is at the same time a specific comprehension linked to the physical body. Shifting between levels of interpretation depends on how *enunciation* (as the emergent *statement*) transforms otherwise disparate phenomenal encounters (denotations) presented by/in the movie. This process privileges the sensory encounter (sight) as the determinate organization of realities prior to their identification *as* typography (understanding via lexical protocols). Foucault focuses interpretation directly on the specific observer whose ability *to see* results in the creation of order. The imposition of a hierarchical conception of power (produced by the cultural roles assigned to the sensory encounter) is constructed from low-level interpretations of *kinetic actions* becoming recognizable expressions of meaning (the 'reading-image').

Robert Able's commercial *Bubbles* (1975) for the beverage 7UP is a prominent, well-known, historical design that engages both *kinesis* and intertextual functions that remain comprehensible. Unlike most TV commercials, this particular design has remained accessible for analysis, giving it an unusual prominence and historical significance. Unlike many contemporary, digitally generated works, this design presents *kinetic actions* that are neither uncanny nor revelations of narrative significance, instead demonstrating a shift between *kinetic* and *graphic* modes as the letters spelling the word "Uncola" extrude [Figure 1.7]. This term was introduced in the successful 1967 advertising campaign[29] that, along with the "See The Light" campaign by Chicago designers Mort and Millie Goldsholl in 1969,[30] provided both text and imagery. *Bubbles* presents imagery to evoke the history of 7UP: the opening imagery of 'bathing beauties' reminds the viewer of the drink's origins in 1929,[31] while the rest of the visuals are from between 1967 and 1974; the butterfly imagery first appeared in the "Butterfly & Bottle" (1969) poster, and the metamorphosis of woman into butterfly that is a climactic image in *Bubbles* appeared in "Uncover Summer" (1970), both by illustrator Pat Dypold. The "See The Light" rainbow was used in a poster by Bill Bosworth from 1973.[32] Variations derived from both illustrators' works appear in Able's design, an intertextual link to the audience's established knowledge of 7UP advertising, giving his visual a familiar, quotational character.

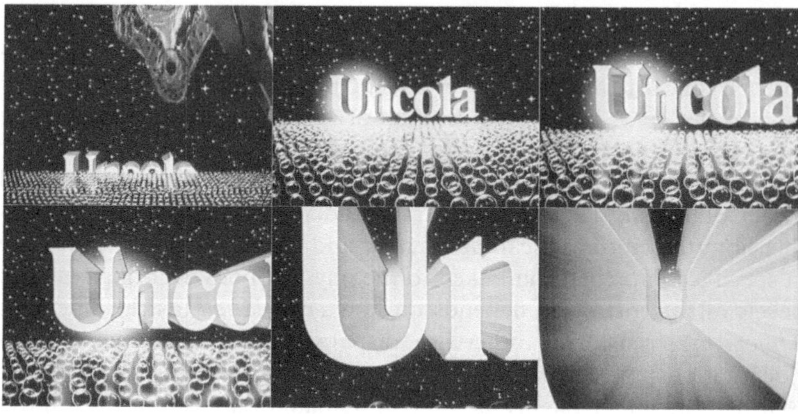

Figure 1.7 The extrusion of "Uncola" and movement through the letter "U" in "Bubbles," designed by Robert Abel (1975)

The 'reading-image' created in the expansion of the letters spelling out "Uncola" as they stretch to become a lengthy 3D form (enabling a camera movement through the tunnel/valley of the "U") has a different valence than the irrationally shifting letters and numbers of Frankfurt's design that implies an expansion of time, a telescoping of distances, a transit across (virtual) space that is a metaphor for a subjective interiority appropriate for the other psychedelic designs and graphics of this commercial. Notably, these shifts and implications were all produced without the digital computer, giving this design a prescient relationship to more contemporary digital animations—hence its value for a consideration of the 'reading-image.' Unlike *Psycho* or *The Number 23*, this visual tunneling is not a graphic representation of madness, but of enlightenment: even though 7UP has not contained the psychoactive element lithium since 1947, the transcendent imagery implies an expansion of consciousness, linking the *kinetic action* and the (emergent) *graphic expression*.

The convergence of these modes poses no difficulties for analysis or interpretation. Differences between *kinetic action*, *graphic expression*, and *chronic progression* are based in their affective role for the audience—their individuality is an artifact of their examination, rather than a necessary and sufficient condition for their separation. The pseudo-independence of these modes depends on audience recognitions that separate individual expressions within a range of other expressive elements simultaneously present within a motion picture—much like the identification of the title sequence. The consolidation of this hybrid example serves to reveal and comment upon mental activity, making it visible as the *activity* of the letterforms themselves. This connection of thought processes to the visuality of the text reverses the normative order where letterforms once identified assume a singular identity and cease to signify through their graphic, imagistic form. This shift from grouping into fragmentation reverses what Saussure identified as foundational for semiosis, yet retains the continuity of encounter that is Foucault's 'enunciative function.' The 'reading-image' brings this dynamic of visuality::legibility into consciousness through its reversion to lower levels of engagement to create a different, parallel signification. The active, performative dimension of movement articulates meaning via a durative product that is not the same as the 'visual manipulations' done on a static page. The perceptual encounter with these transformations extends enunciation/articulation to what are purely and innately visual constructs. Unlike the *metaphor* of 'sequence' in a static design—where all the elements are always necessarily immanent in the composition—the simple fact of *time* in a motion graphic work means that what appears on-screen is not necessarily a fixed feature of the design; with all static designs, it must be (it is the definitional, necessary, and sufficient condition for being 'static'). The tendency to speak of the 'duration of viewing' in a graphic design work is not the same as the temporal dimension ('running time') of a motion graphic, which is modulated in ways that the fixed immanence of static design is not; to suggest otherwise is a common fallacy that conflates mutually exclusive conditions in a reification of metaphor. *Kinetic actions* are specific, additional motions shown by motion typography, distinguished from the more general motion and development in time on-screen. Their discreteness from all the other active dimensions of animated text serves an enunciative role—a second utterance—that accompanies, comments upon, and expands the range of signification for motion typography. These dimensions are particular to motion pictures, entirely and completely different than what can be produced with static compositions—fixed positions and unchanging signification—in graphic design.

Notes

1 Krasner, J. *Motion Graphic Design: Applied History and Aesthetics, Third Edition* (New York: Focal Press, 2013).
2 Schyns, P. G. "Categories and percepts: a bi-directional framework for categorization" *Trends in Cognitive Sciences* vol. 1, no. 5. (August 1997) pp. 183–189.
3 Foucault, M. *The Archaeology of Knowledge* (New York: Pantheon, 1972) p. 88.
4 Deleuze, G. *Cinema 1: The Movement-Image* (Minneapolis: University of Minnesota Press, 1986) p. ix.

5 Deleuze, G. *Cinema 1: The Movement-Image* (Minneapolis: The University of Minnesota Press, 1989) np.
6 Deleuze, G. *Cinema 2: The Time-Image* (Minneapolis: The University of Minnesota Press, 1989) pp. 25–26.
7 Betancourt, M. *The Critique of Digital Capitalism* (Brooklyn: Punctum Books, 2016) pp. 153–190.
8 Betancourt, M. *The History of Motion Graphics: From Avant-Garde to Industry in the United States* (Rockport: Wildside Press, 2013).
9 Spigel, L. "Back to the Drawing Board: Graphic Design and the Visual Environment of Television at Midcentury" *Cinema Journal* vol. 55, no. 4. (Summer 2016) pp. 28–54.
10 Haskin, P. and Bass, S. "'Saul, Can You Make Me a Title?': Interview with Saul Bass" *Film Quarterly* vol. 50, no. 1. (Autumn 1996) p. 12.
11 Modley, R. "Graphic Symbols for World-Wide Communication" *Sign Image Symbol* György Kepes (New York: George Braziller, 1966) pp. 108–133.
12 Ducharte, P. L. *The Italian Comedy: The Improvisation, Scenarios, Lives, Attributes, Portraits and Masks of the Illustrious Characters of the Commedia dell'Arte* (New York: Dover, 1966) p. 17.
13 Kincaid, Z. *Kabuki: The Popular Stage of Japan* (London: MacMillan, 1925) pp. 21–22.
14 Betancourt, M. *Semiotics and Title Sequences: Text–Image Composites in Motion Graphics* (New York: Routledge Focus, 2017) pp. 31–33.
15 Beck, J. ed. "#38" *The 50 Greatest Cartoons* (Atlanta: Turner Publishing, 1994) pp. 154–155.
16 Bernard, J. *The Fifty Greatest Cartoon as Selected by 1,000 Animation Professional* (Atlanta: Turner Publishing, 1994) p. 55.
17 Caws, M. *The Surrealist Painters and Poets: An Anthology* (Cambridge: The MIT Press, 2001) pp. 179.
18 Foucault, M. *The Archaeology of Knowledge* (New York: Pantheon, 1972).
19 Sharits, P. "Several Premises on 'Assumptions' and How They Free the Writer" *I Was a Flawed Modernist* ed. Sarah Markgraf (New York: The New American Cinema Group/The Film-maker's Coop, 2017) p. 9.
20 "Process Philosophy" *Stanford Encyclopedia of Philosophy* website plato.stanford.edu/entries/process-philosophy/ revision October 26, 2017 retrieved May 1, 2018.
21 Foucault, M. *The Birth of the Clinic* (New York: Vintage, 1975) p. xiii.
22 Rogers, H. "The Musical Script: Norman McLaren, Animated Sound, and Audiovisuality" *Animation Journal* vol. 22. (2014) p. 76.
23 Small, E. *Direct Theory: Experimental Motion Pictures as a Major Genre, Second Edition* (Carbondale: Southern Illinois University Press, 2013) p. 56.
24 Betancourt, M. "Motion Perception in Movies and Paintings: Towards a New Kinetic Art" *CTheory* (October 23, 2002) ctheory.net/articles.aspx?id=349.
25 Saussure, F. *Course in General Linguistics* (New York: 1966) p. 128.
26 Barnett, D. *Movement as Meaning in Experimental Film* (New York: Rodopi, 2008).

27 Hochberg, J. and Brooks, V. "Movies in the Mind's Eye" *Post Theory* ed. David Bordwell and Noel Carroll (Madison: University of Wisconsin Press, 1996) pp. 368–369.
28 Foucault, M. *The Birth of the Clinic* (New York: Vintage, 1975) p. xiii.
29 "Cadbury Schweppes, America's Beverages: 7Up, the Making of a Legend" *Brands People Love* website, April 30, 2008, retrieved April 29, 2018 web.archive.org/web/20080430022917/brandspeoplelove.com/csab/?TabId=148
30 Beste, A. "Designers in Film: Goldsholl Design Associates" *Light Industry* website, December 8, 2015, retrieved April 29, 2018 lightindustry.org/goldsholl
31 "Cadbury Schweppes, America's Beverages: 7Up, the Making of a Legend" *Brands People Love* website, April 30, 2008, retrieved April 29, 2018 web.archive.org/web/20080430022917/brandspeoplelove.com/csab/?TabId=148
32 Hix, L. "An Un-Conventional Thirst: Collecting 7Up's Most Beautiful, Hallucinatory Billboards" *Collector's Weekly* website, August 31, 2016, retrieved April 29, 2018 collectorsweekly.com/articles/collecting-7ups-most-beautiful-hallucinatory-billboards/

2 Graphic Expression

Typography is a hybrid, a visual form whose visuality is negated in the act of reading. Graphic design institutionalized this negation, masking the imagistic character of text through Modernist concerns with legibility: the minimization of visual ambivalence that can render a text unintelligible.[1] As visual expression immanently becomes the lexical interpretation, a product that is *reading*—the animated typo/graphy of motion graphics develops from this historical context familiar from static design in two ways that are not mutually exclusive: [a] as letterforms themselves; [b] as imagistic elements appearing on-screen, but which are *not* type.[2] The capacity to *become* typography or image, as when letterforms disintegrate into pixel dust (thus assuming a new, independent identity as graphics that are *not* typography and cannot be confused with it), fundamentally separates animated typo/graphics from graphic design: *any* movement, even superficially 'stationary' actions (rotation, pulsation, vibration, color changes, as well as animorphs) are transformative. Recognizing and engaging with these ambivalences reveals linked issues of reading and perception that constrain audience interpretive expectation/engagement with text (its identity as letterforms, pictograms, or ideograms), a convergence of graphic design and motion graphics that paradoxically marks their differences as a direct product of *animation*. Legibility (formal design), expectation (past experience), and anticipation (subjective encounter) behave in divergent ways when describing static or motion typography. The additional meanings given by *kinesis* that accompany typo/graphics reflect this cultural expertise and medium-dependence,[3] not simply the immanent perception of what appears on-screen. The identification 'typography' is simultaneously an ordering of experience that renders it meaningful *as* language following a primary category assignment: superficially positioned *before* any particular statement or meaning, this domain membership[4] establishes all engagements within ranges of potential *prior* to their higher-level signification, thus exhibiting the "gignomenological law of identity,"[5] where initial decisions about *identity* are ratified by their later utility: any further category evaluation is halted, and further decisions about potential correspondences are no longer generated from the flux of experience once the identification "typography" has been made. The shifts between language and image, recognition and abstraction that define the 'reading-image' are apparent in the development and emergence *into being-typography* made possible by *kinesis.* Recognizing imagery as *being-language* does not depend on legibility or intelligibility (past experience) since *poetic* visuals, and even unknown languages such as hieroglyphics, are still comprehended as *being-language*, an identification learned via past experience and encompassing all of its possible results.[6] This intransigent category assignment in static design creates the belief in an ontological identity for type, that what is type *always* remains type (true for static designs). This belief is a fallacy for moving designs. When what seems like an essential ontological status, "typography," reveals itself as an interpretation, a conclusion, it becomes amenable to plastic deformation and manipulation. Extricating motion from static typography depends on audience response, not to this contingency, but to the literal *conversion* of typography by *kinesis*: precisely those identities manipulated in the 'reading-image.'

The reading of stylized ("art") typefaces described by semiotician Hartmut Stóckl in his article "Typography: Body and Dress of a Text" reveals the importance of visuality (*graphics*) in parsing the appearance of all text. Visuality informs the emotive dimensions of meaning, communicating an Expressionist excess beyond the lexical:

> Typefaces may point to the nature of the document, carry emotional values or indicate the writer's intended audience, and aspects of the layout may serve to reinforce the thematic structure of a given text and facilitate access to its information. Finally, on yet another level of typographic meaning making, the graphic signs of writing can assume pictorial qualities. Thus, letters may form visual shapes which stand for objects from reality, signal states-of-affairs or actions, and illustrate emotions. Materials and techniques of graphic sign making, too, may be made salient in text design and can thus convey something about the situation, genre and stylistic intent of a communicative occurrence—this is also a pictorial kind of communication. It is this threefold semiotic nature of typography that provides its communicative flexibility.[7]

These familiar relationships between type design and lexical meaning unite motion typography with static design, giving *graphic expressions* a descriptive potential beyond motion graphics; only *kinesis* makes the 'reading-image.' The interpretation of "visual shapes which stand for objects from reality, signal states-of-affairs or actions, and illustrate emotions" gives these engagements with language as a graphic material a familiar form apparent in historical developments with visual or concrete poetry, and demonstrating the centrality of enculturation.[8] The differentiation of written language (lexicality) from image (visuality) is an assignment of encultured meaning to the abstraction of markings. There are significant overlaps in the ambivalent comprehension of words and meaning in both static and motion designs, a function of *how* the text appears. In those instances where images are simultaneously typography or contain elements that combine to become typography—*skeuomorphic* graphics—the letterforms are either composed from recognizable imagery that *is* both letterforms and pictures, or when taken as a gestalt *becomes* letterforms, but which simultaneously retain their independent identities as smaller, readily identified pictures (see Figure 2.11, page 92). Lexical understanding is learning when to apply the appropriate rules (*langue*) to use these systems (*semiosis*): the reader internalizes this hierarchy as a dominant force delivered through visual perception. These simultaneous critical and material enculturations of both lexical and non-lexical forms are an established dynamic unmasked by the 'reading-image' performing on-screen (the mode of *graphic expression*).

Surveying avant-garde experiments with typography throughout the twentieth century articulates a consistent approach to the imagery forming kinetic *graphic expressions*. French avant-garde praxis from the 1890s through World War I was dominated by these concerns, both in art publications and in popular design, apparent from the transformation of letterforms in Art Nouveau designs to be expressive as well as informative, demonstrating Arts and Crafts designer William Morris's influence on *fin-de-siècle* typography.[9] These visual dimensions of typography and layout were systematically suppressed by the Constructivist innovation of "graphic design" in the 1920s.[10] The difference between 'legible typography' and 'graphic visuals' arises simultaneously as parallel, independent engagements in *reading* and *seeing*, a shifting of interpretive modes that happens fluently and instantly when considering text–image composites, but which is in flux, delayed, or ambivalent in *graphic expressions*.

Visuality::legibility enables a consideration of the other semiotic elements of on-screen text, apart from letterforms and their variable identity-roles in motion typography. Typographer and design theorist Johanna Drucker describes these possibilities in her discussion of graphics and their *narrative function* in static designs for books and other print publications:

> Within the larger task of interpretation (our work as critics, scholars and teachers) we can read ideological, cultural and historical

> matters in these graphic dimensions and the way they structure subject positions from which telling unfolds and within narrative is constrained and structured. I would go farther and say that certain assumptions, values and beliefs can only be accessed through critical reading of these devices.[11]

Acknowledging the expressive potentials posed by non-lexical graphics makes their semiosis and interpretive activity possible; this recognition unites graphic design and motion graphics in separating typography from non-typography. Without the initial recognition that simple graphics can also signify without *being-type*, and carry particular cultural values that parallel other dimensions of lexical form, the analysis and consideration of those elements that might seem "decorative" is futile: it is a matter of including these parts of the design within the horizons of interpretation.

The problem with theorizing typography that Drucker has repeatedly identified is the general lack of critical and philosophical consideration it has received;[12] the study of language and signification in semiotics, media theory, and philosophy disembodies type as a dematerialized essence, numinous, expressing a realm 'beyond' human sensory encounter.[13] Considering the physical nature of letterforms and their arrangement leads to an embodied engagement with the expressive capacities in/of typography, its visuality, a theorization that requires attention not only to the immanence of the design, but to its morphology and structure in relation to historical art, especially the work of the literary avant-garde, rather than only as a work of graphic design; understanding *graphic expressions* requires a historical approach that links the role of *kinesis* to the static organization of visuality.

Fragmented and de/composed text, which can be readily identified as typography but is illegible or otherwise unreadable, has been a common feature of avant-garde art that includes typography and lettering throughout the twentieth century. This approach forces viewers to acknowledge the graphic nature of text, using its recognition as language to transform the legible back into the visual, reversing the familiar hierarchy of *reading–seeing–hearing*. Industrial film director Francis Thompson's "city symphony"[14] film *N. Y., N. Y.* (1958) contains shots with partially legible, but always identifiable, typography in the 'night-life' sequence at the end of the film [Figure 2.1]. The optical distortion of lettering that creates a polar coordinate displacement of the credits in Kyle Cooper's title design for *Sphere* (1998) employs the same type of optical distortions that Thompson employs throughout *N. Y., N. Y.* to create a fluid transmogrification of imagery; similar distortions of the credit texts are uncommon, notably used in Maurice Binder's James Bond title sequences of the 1960s, starting with *Thunderball* (1965), but

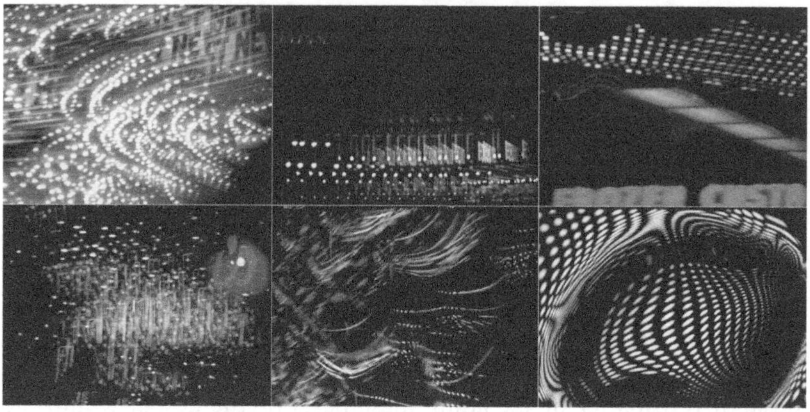

Figure 2.1 Stills from the 'nightlife' sequence in *N. Y., N. Y.* (1958) by Francis Thompson

occasionally also appearing in contemporary designs such as *Spawn* (1998) or *Across the Universe* (2007), both by Kyle Cooper, or in the main title card designed by Richard Greenberg for *Star Trek: Nemesis* (2002). Optical transformations more typically simply blur the text through defocusing rather than distortion, making the optical effects appearing in these designs strikingly similar despite the very great differences between the movies themselves.

Graphic expressions in particular illustrate the dynamic connections between visuality and lexicality. While the text in Thompson's design loses its legibility by being distorted, the credits in Cooper's designs do not. The transformative capacity of *graphic expressions* extends outside the realm of text, with the same category of optical distortions appearing in avant-garde films such as Ira Cohen's *The Invasion of Thunderbolt Pagoda* (1968), where sheets of acetate distort and warp figures, or in the self-consciously digital manipulations of the commercial music video *Corporate Cannibal* (2009) by Nick Hooker [Figure 2.2].[15] The juxtaposition of realism into abstraction transforms the live action imagery of all these movies into *graphics*. The indistinction of source and digital processing is apparent in these designs, as Steven Shaviro noted in his discussion of the visual transmutations of singer Grace Jones in *Corporate Cannibal*:

> The video works by continually manipulating Grace Jones' figure. In the course of the song's six minutes and eight seconds, this figure swells and contracts, bends and fractures, twists, warps, and

> contorts, and flows from one shape to another. [...] In spite of all these distortions, Jones remains recognizable throughout. [...] Even as it melts and scatters Jones' features, it retains their abrasive angular uniqueness. In the course of the video's manipulations of her image, Jones' appearance loses all identity; it is never "the same" from one moment to the next. And yet her figure continues to insistently confront us. As we hear her voice on the soundtrack, her lips and voice hold our visual attention.[16]

Synchronized sound, as Shaviro notes, has a decisive role in maintaining the recognition of Jones across the multiple and varied transformations, providing the same referential anchor that the identification of/as type provides in *N. Y., N. Y.*: her image may distort and mutate into spidery, compressed, tortured figures, all mouth and teeth, resembling the Surrealist works of Hans Bellmer, Max Ernst, or the monster in *Three Studies for a Crucifixion* (1944) by Francis Bacon, yet she remains *Grace Jones* throughout these shifts, readily identified by the synchronization and its conventional association of sound and image. Although these mutations are specifically digital, they recall the earlier fluidity of animated morphs,[17] returning these uncanny digital distortions and optical effects to the more familiar realms of the avant-garde, motion graphics, and VFX. In emphasizing the visuality of the image, *graphic expressions* return typography to a more basic ambivalence where visual identifications—as *being-type*, as *being-figure* (Jones)—demand the audience acknowledge that their understanding is always contingent on externalities to what they see, recognitions arising from past experience.

The 'texts' in *N. Y., N. Y.* are derived from physical phenomena. These lit-up signs are not always legible because of the kaleidoscopic distortion, but they are immediately recognizable as *being-typography*, even though the letterforms are partial and the words they form do not consistently appear on-screen. Historically only animation commonly presents such fluid transmogrifications of imagery,[18] but its difference—*being-animation*—indicates a divergent domain whose expectations did not *normally* apply to (historical) live action motion pictures. The presentations in Thompson's film are thus exceptional, an outlier that explores what *graphic expressions* do with/to live action materials, and so anticipates the developments of digital animation in Hooker's video. The emotive dimensions of the distortions dominate the text's presentation-reception. The conversion from type into image is nearly complete. These 'reading-images' demonstrate that semiotician Roman Jakobson's discussion of the *poetic function* is not limited to verbal form. His attention to non-linguistic modifications of meaning, such as expressions of emotion, complicates the interpretations offered by semiosis:

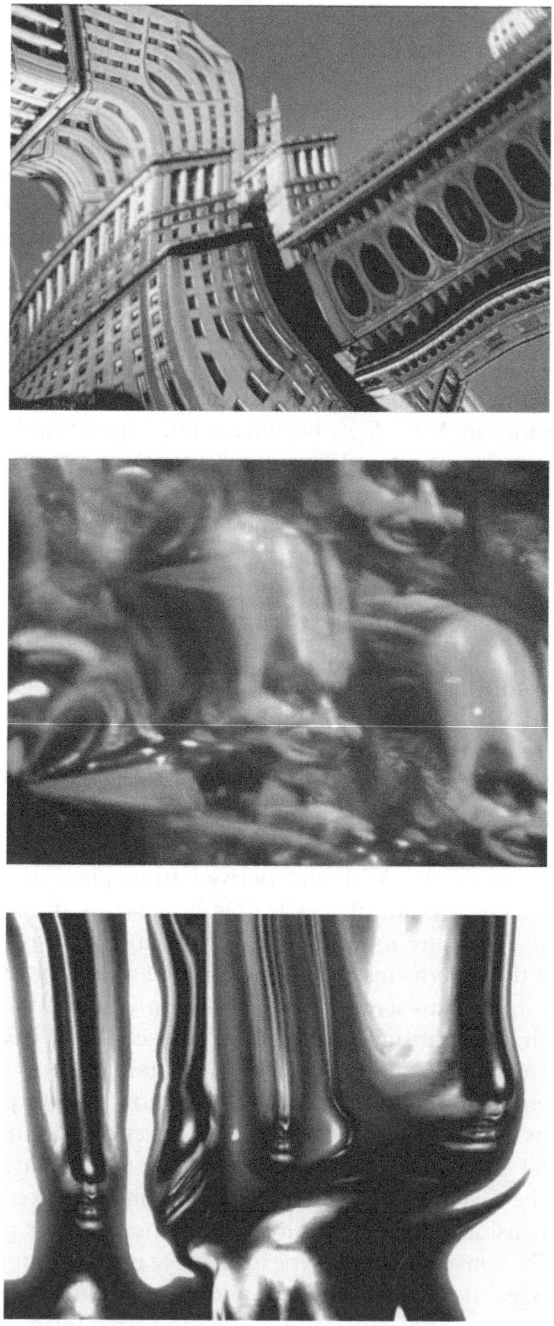

Figure 2.2 Stills showing optical distortions in [Top] Francis Thompson, *N. Y., N. Y.* (1958); [Middle] Ira Cohen, *The Invasion of Thunderbolt Pagoda* (1968); [Bottom] Nick Hooker, *Corporate Cannibal* (2008)

> The set (*Einstellung*) toward the *message* as such, focus on the message for its own sake, is the *poetic* function of language. [...] This function, by promoting the palpability of signs, deepens the fundamental dichotomy of signs and objects.[19]

The opposition between signs and the materials that form them is suspended in Jakobson's *poetic function* as an indeterminacy where the non-lexical dominates the interpretation of the lexical—in poetry the sound of the words is as important or more important than what they mean. He proposes this function as a specialized problem of verbal structure where the emotive significance inflects utterances, giving and altering meaning on the phonic, grammatical, and lexical levels.[20] However, his proposal does not consider typography, nor design, leaving the written form of language outside his analysis; neither does he interrogate *legibility* in the rigorous fashion apparent in how he addressed the rhetorics of grammar generating *poeisis*. Typo/graphics were outside his area of interest. Whatever expressive affects and modifications type and layout offer to meaning are implied, but not considered; only by extending his analysis beyond the verbalization of language does the design itself become a source of meaning. While every graphic designer is aware of these impacts (it is the foundational recognition defining their field), the contributions of typo/graphics have been systematically excluded from consideration: affects accruing to typefaces, their placement, and the designed composition all correspond to these same enunciative redirections of significance produced as visual parallels to verbalized speech. The momentary recognitions of lettering in *N. Y., N. Y.* anchors the more abstract and partial signage, transforming even the most illegible, abstract patterns into potential language. Because the audience knows *what* these patterns originate with, their identity links them to the graphics and formal qualities of text. The typo/graphics in Thompson's use of signage parallels those employed by Walker Evans in *Times Square / Broadway Composition* (1930), a photograph that composited multiple lighted signs to create a graphic collage that remains legible [Figure 2.3]—while Thompson's film suggests Cubo-Futurist compositions in motion. This fragmentation renders the film's letterforms *purely* graphic, a motion collage of shards and suggestions of text and textuality, which the audience nevertheless recognizes and understands without legibility becoming a concern. This same understanding anchors the text distortions in *Sphere*. Abstracted shots act as cyphers for their more familiar contents, a symbolic allusion to 'nightlife' in *N. Y., N. Y.* which develops more explicitly in the sequence that follows. Unlike 'asemic typography' that lacks both legibility and semiosis,[21] these word fragments are understood as graphic symbols *representing* signage. *Any* language they *might* contain is simply an

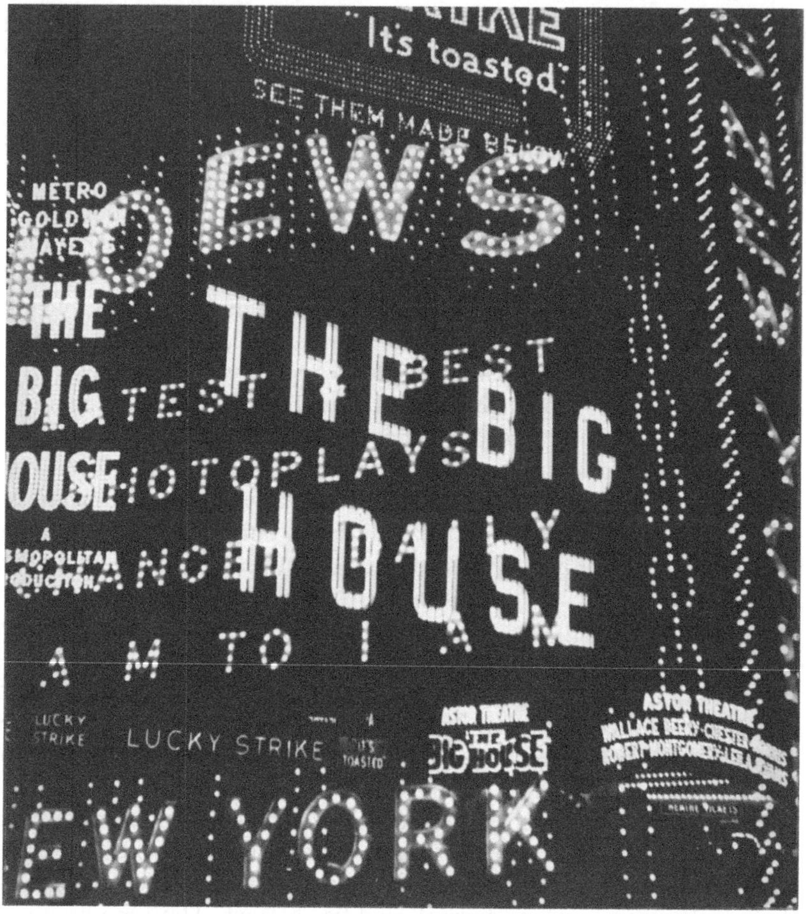

Figure 2.3 J. Paul Getty Museum, Los Angeles
Walker Evans, "Times Square / Broadway Composition," 1930, photograph, 24.8 × 21.7 cm (9 3/4 × 8 9/16 in.)

irrelevant dimension of their pictorial role in the film. These texts create a non-lexical 'reading-image' where the significance of the graphic patterns as representations of 'words' supplants the semiosis that actual words would necessarily produce: the identification of the fragmentary and glimpsed letterforms is sufficient to convey the meaning 'signage at night.' This recognition then becomes the significance of the image, rather than reading the signs as particular identifiers naming specific businesses. In offering a 'generalized' depiction of language, these photographs stand in for any sign, for any business, anywhere in the city, rather than automatically locating somewhere particular. In making this distinction, their abstractions offer an experience about 'reading' and identifying that rarely occurs in reality: a specific encounter with the non-specific, something that typically can only happen through the abstract *discourse* of language, *not* through the always identified and uniquely located views offered in pictures, or the precise demarcations stated by text. These graphics behave linguistically, yet retain the superficial indexicality of photographs.

Paradoxically, the role of language during this section of *N. Y., N. Y.* serves as a rupture that makes the dominance of visuality also a denial of its *non*-lexical status. Approaching text pictorially determines its meaning: images of incomprehensibly fragmented typography/graphics that are language. Their form is both purely pictorial and necessarily abstracted from their ontological, pro-filmic sources, a significance separate from reading *and* from the recognitions of realist photography, but which retains its indexicality. When reading, letters do not determine the meaning for the words they form, yet in these shots that is precisely what happens, their interpretations shifting between pictorial depiction and language-fragment. These problematics are precisely why these images are of interest: they offer an encapsulated instance of what the 'reading-image' looks like when it is not immediately concerned with text. This semiotic process entails a transfer determined not only by legibility, but by visuality (the role of *kinesis* in composition and presentation).

This expanded field of consideration for typo/graphic expressions, however, raises ideological and conceptual issues for existing Modern and Post-Modern theories developed in the twentieth century, and its aftermath, the theories of the Contemporary in the twenty-first.[22] These are fundamental issues of appropriateness and approach that Drucker has specifically addressed as problematics for considering the work of graphic design in a larger context, whether historical or theoretical:

> The history and critical discussion of modern art developed with European innovation in abstraction and the avant-garde at its core has never been able to find a place in its arguments for those visual works that figured their engagement with Modern life through representational imagery or an enthusiastic dialogue with the mass media. Yet such work is irrefutably modern in its visual forms and requires a theoretical discussion that considers the relation between fine art and mass culture in its vernacular, popular and commercial manifestations.[23]

Written in 1999, Drucker's comments are still appropriate almost twenty years later: the challenges posed by a 'visual culture' approach to the historical avant-garde continue to find resistance not only within art history, but in the realm of cinema as well. The dearth of studies engaging this heritage of *commercial design-fine art-cinema* overlap is immediately obvious when confronting the motion graphics field (even more than in graphic design)—a strange development, since the connections between popular and elite culture are especially apparent in the role of abstraction and avant-garde film for title sequences in feature films (as 'avant-pop'). Intertextual connections between commercial film design and abstract film bring the expressive potential of the typo/graphics of *N. Y., N. Y.* into view, dramatizing the dialogue between the mass media (commercial cinema) and avant-garde cinema. These relationships are especially apparent in the Early Phase of the Designer Period between 1954 and 1963, when graphic designers such as Saul Bass and Maurice Binder began producing credit sequences for films that adapted the imagery of their Modernist advertising posters into animated titles.[24] These transfers of Modern design to commercial titling were not unanticipated, radical innovations, since designer/publisher Merle Armitage had already applied Modernist principles to the titles of films such as *Song of the Thin Man* (1947) nearly a decade earlier.[25]

In these new approaches to film title design, the compositions feature not only text, but a variety of graphic elements that complement the layout. The role and importance of non-photographic elements in Saul Bass's title sequence for *The Man With The Golden Arm* (1955) shows how *kinesis* provides a complementary counterpoint to the presence and organization of typography. The white lines of Bass's design evoke the animated rectangles of Hans Richter's film *Rhythmus 21* (aka *Film ist Rhythmus*, 1921/23) [Figure 2.4], believed in the 1950s[26] to be the earliest of the German "Absolute Films" produced in the 1920s.[27] There is no deformation of the signified meaning. The intertextual recognition of these graphic lines as a quotation of Richter's film is not a product of their linkage to the texts on-screen, nor does it alter the meaning of that written information: it is a pure excess, apart from the linguistic, a quotation that transforms the significance of the design as a whole without altering its lexical content. These dimensions of quotation and graphic significance are entirely distinct from the role of text::image combinations that act as a rebus,[28] and whose meaning depends on knowing the narrative to evoke this material as metonymic with heroin addiction, thus explaining the drift into audio-visual syncopation and identifying these lines as "needles." Instead, the *graphic expression* offers a parallel enunciation to this intratextual *narrative function* that modulates and transforms the signification process, redirecting the meaning elsewhere: the visual form cannot be separated from the *graphic expression*.

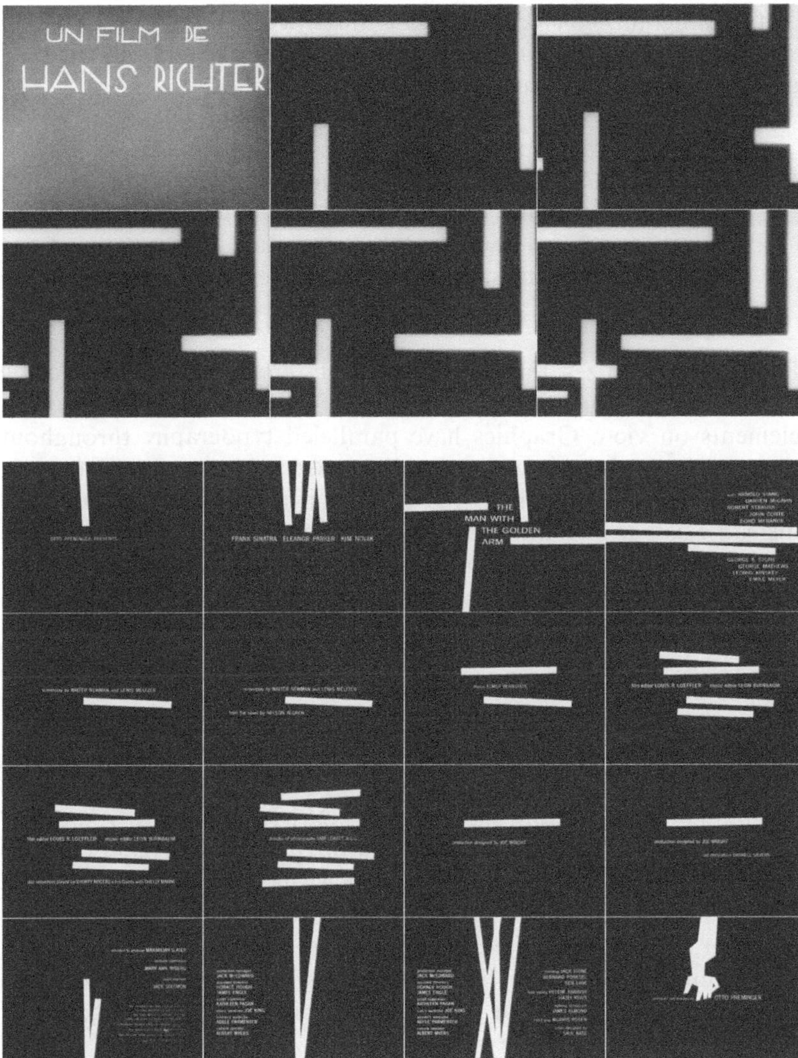

Figure 2.4 [Top] Stills from the end of *Rhythmus 21* (*Film ist Rhythmus*, 1921/23) by Hans Richter, showing the influence of his film in [Bottom] all the title cards for *The Man With The Golden Arm* (1955), designed by Saul Bass

The graphic dimension of textuality typically remains 'invisible' unless it interferes with legibility or calls attention to itself,[29] as the signage does in *N. Y., N. Y.* This dismissal of the visual character demonstrates the dynamics and hierarchy in reading::seeing that

Michel Foucault explained in the book *This is not a Pipe*. His analysis of the calligrams created in/by René Magritte's paintings describes an approach to language as a visual material whose conventional reading is always potentially in question:

> For the text to shape itself, for all its juxtaposed signs to form a dove, a flower, a rainstorm, the gaze must refrain from any possible reading. Letters must remain points, sentences lines, paragraphs surfaces or masses—wings, stalks, or petals. The text must say nothing to this gazing subject who is a viewer, not a reader. As soon as he begins to read, in fact, shape dissipates.[30]

Foucault recognizes that writing and its engagement *as* linguistic subsumes its visuality in the process of assigning meaning to the elements on view. Graphics have paralleled typography throughout their use in motion pictures, providing a second level of signification: because this relationship is *not* an all-or-nothing proposition, but instead exists in a continuum between those texts that are so insistently visual that their legibility disappears, and other texts where legibility is so dominant that the graphic, visual character becomes irrelevant to their consideration. The modulation and manipulation of these dimensions of *kinesis* within this dynamic range defines the specific action involved in apprehending and understanding visual poetry. The cross-shaped mask [Figure 2.5] that appears during the opening of *Stella Maris* (1918) to introduce Mary Pickford's parallel role of "Unity Blake," who lives in a "London orphanage," acts as a framing device, setting the building apart from the other shots of the opening, but also behaves informationally, as a statement that this orphanage is run by the Church. It is an easily comprehended graphic whose function as *imagistic* signifier has precisely the same linguistic function as the fragmented typography in *N. Y., N. Y.* Being static, its meaning emerges not from the mask's motion, but through the sequential arrangement of its images—a product of montage rather than an immanent feature of *kinesis*.

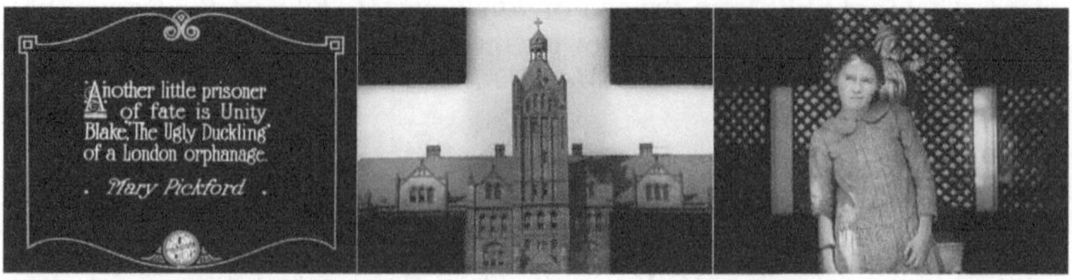

Figure 2.5 Cross-shaped mask from the opening to *Stella Maris* (1919)

The category assignments that make a work *narrative* or *non-narrative*, *realist* or *abstract*, each provides a different set of encultured guides that act in the same way that deciding an image is *type* does: they direct and constrain interpretation in particular, predictable ways. The development of "cryptographic fonts" such as graphic designer Sang Mun's *Z-X-X* typeface (2012) reveals the link between concerns with visuality and the intelligibility that is essential to reading, through attempts to produce a typeface that can confuse an automated system such as a digital computer's ability to capture and recognize text. One variant of this typeface involves the doubling of letters, one large and prominently legible, the other smaller and in close proximity to the larger letter, while another variant addresses the 'problem' of machine reading by inserting 'noise' into the text to contrast with its lexicality. Both cryptographic variants make the invisible decision-process of human reading a conscious act of decipherment. Both the doubling of letterforms and the integration of illegible noise increase the ambivalence of the reading process, rendering the typeface itself either difficult to discern or by confusing the significant letters via displacement.

These same dynamics are active in Maurice Binder's title sequence for *Arabesque* (1966), which makes this fluid shifting of typo/graphics an explicit feature of the design [Figure 2.6]. This instrumental process is concerned with interpreting the visual forms or shapes apart from the linguistic contents; in practice, this shifting from graphic to lexical is the 'transparency' of text that is essential to its legibility. Familiar technical processes such as video feedback (what the BBC engineers called "howlaround") have a dramatic effect on typography, as Binder's design demonstrates. The recursive process transforms text into the graphic patterns that spiral and repeat on-screen. In his memoir, *Ben at the Beeb*, BBC engineer Ben Palmer recalled his work with creating the video feedback that appears in this design:

> Another way to initiate the oscillation was to feed a separate picture to the monitor, as well as that from the camera. This picture then provided the trigger points for the feedback effect and all these patterns and blobs of light then appeared to emanate from the bright parts of the picture. [...] Norman Taylor, the man who first noticed this effect, used it on one or two shows, to produce a dream effect. But the use that everyone has seen was on the opening titles of *Dr. Who*. [...] One of the leading Titles men in the Film industry, Maurice Binder, heard somehow about this work and came to see me at the Studios. [...] He wanted something different for a film called *Arabesque* and I showed him what we could do. He chose the stark black and white effects of phase reversal. The BBC gave permission for their equipment to be used for a commercial

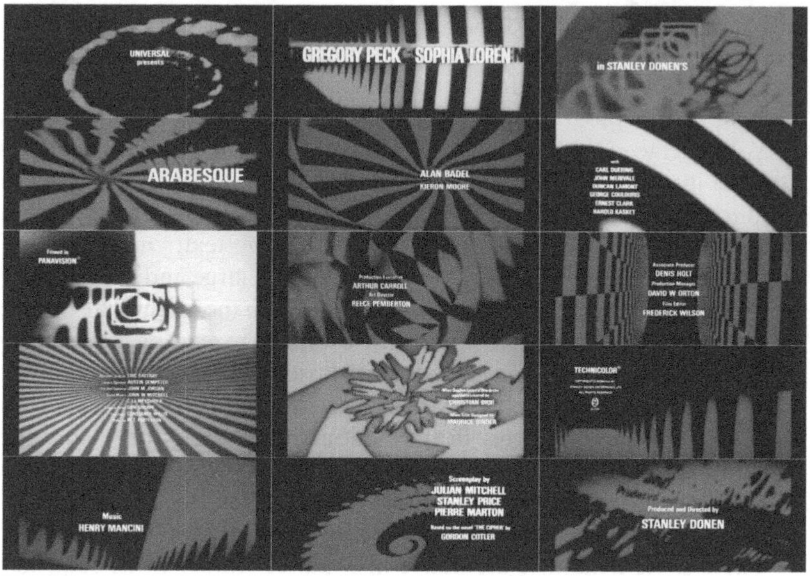

Figure 2.6 All the title cards in *Arabesque* (1966), designed by Maurice Binder

> film—a very great novelty in those days! So we shot it on 35mm telerecording and Maurice took it away, amazed at how little the BBC had charged him for this facility.[31]

Arabesque displays dynamic shifts from legibility into illegibility that do not prevent the recognition of these graphics as simultaneously *being-typography*. Recognizing that the same text appears in the background as in the white, superimposed credit ensures the audience will interpret these patterns as a transformation of typography. The links between graphics and typography depends on their shared visual nature: using the same Kodalith transparencies employed in the optical printing masks to make the video feedback means these distorted texts remain legible. As with Mun's proposals for *Z-X-X* and the distortions in *N. Y., N. Y.*, Binder's design employs ambivalence expressively, as camouflage to hide contents *without* becoming incomprehensible. They remain within the familiar domain of recognizable texts, but are not primarily engaged with legibility as was common for Modernist approaches to graphic design. In shifting attention to the actions of decipherment—the process of identifying and reading the characters themselves repeating in the feedback, or in the arrangement of *Z-X-X*—they reveal *en passant* the centrality of encultured expectations in governing and organizing text apart from its graphic nature. *Graphic expressions* depend on instabilities between text and image for their affect: the 'reading-image' converts this reflexivity of abstraction and familiar language into fluid, immanent dimensions of the lexical encounter, rather than discrete and otherwise independent activities.

The same shifting of typo/graphics appears in Stan VanDerBeek and Kenneth Knowlton's *Poemfield* series, employing a graphic treatment of simplified letterforms. These computer-generated films made at Bell Labs in their Artist in Residency program between 1966 and 1972 all employ the digital computer to generate and transform words into shifting and repeating patterns that remain recognizable as lettering throughout their transformations, but quickly lose legibility to become a 'field' of letter and word fragments, as shown in Figure 2.7. This pioneering computer animation anticipates similar developments with generative digital systems and experimental digital typography starting in the 1980s. The *Poemfields* series established a precedent developed in videos such as Norbert Meissner's *Pfingsten* (1989), where fragments of religious texts gradually become coherent, or in the static designs of April Grieman and David Carson, where legibility is not the central concern of the design. Media historian Gloria Sutton explains these typo/graphics in her study on VanDerBeek's work:

> While the medium of *Poemfield No. 2* is 16 mm film, its operations are not bound up with the self-reflexive machinations of the cinematic apparatus, neither in terms of calling attention to the institution of cinema nor the psychological dynamics at play within spectatorship. *Poemfield No. 2*'s formal experiments with poetry and film are in dialogue with an altogether different and earlier set of concerns, what György Kepes famously described in 1944 as "visual communication."[32]

The dynamic process of becoming-coherent, central to Kepes's proposal, is the focus of the *Poemfield* films. This ambivalency distinguishes visual semiosis from the bounded nature of lexical form. The dynamics of enunciation and comprehension make this initial identification of typography essential to its decomposition into pixels and repeating black fragments in a process that anticipates the isolation and decompositions common to similar transformations: the realization of alternatives—a *heterotopia*—is disruptive and problematic, identifying how discourse is a reflection of an underlying hierarchy and systemic order.[33] The same 'dream effect' of flowing video feedback visuals in the titles created by Norman Taylor and designed by Bernard Lodge for *Doctor Who* (1963–1973) that Palmer discussed, or how the pictorial contents turn into digital graphics in glitch art videos such as Takeshi Murata's

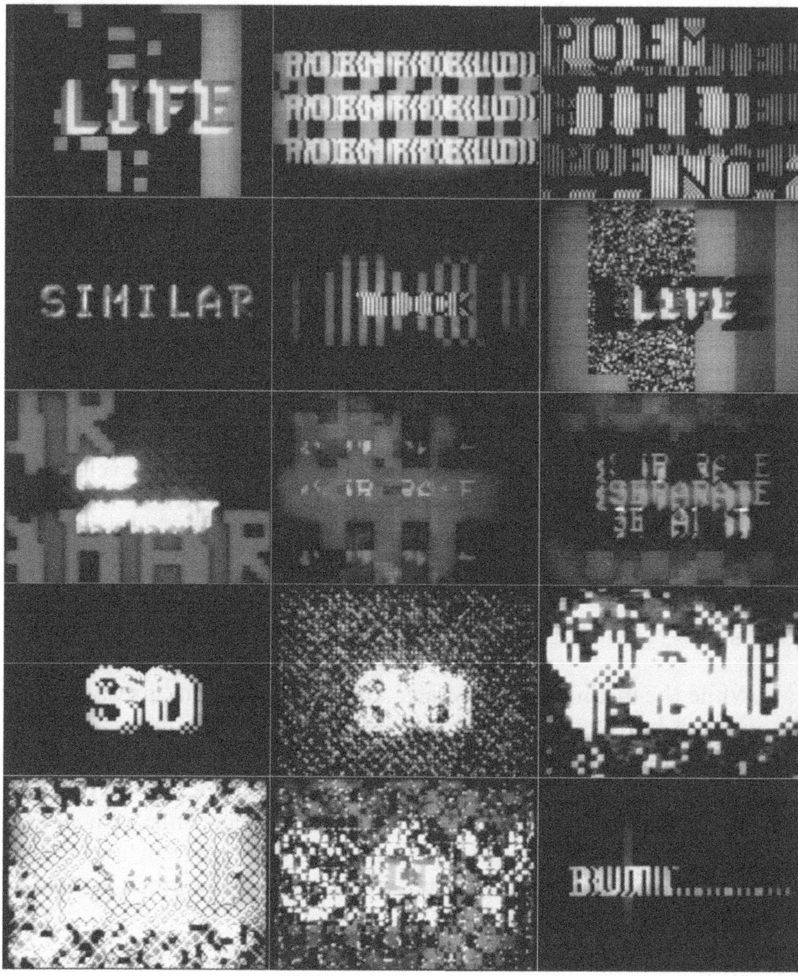

Figure 2.7 Selected stills from *Poemfield No. 2* (1966–1971) by Stan VanDerBeek and Kenneth Knowlton, produced at Bell Labs in Murray Hill, NJ

Monster Movie (2005),[34] reveal the same blocky break-up of the picture that appears in the manipulations of the *Poemfield* films [Figure 2.8]. Sutton noted that these concerns with recognition and comprehension are more closely aligned with the approaches of graphic design—and its Modernist concern with legibility—than with the materialist concerns common to avant-garde film in the 1960s, making the link between works such as *Poemfield No. 2* and *Arabesque* (thus, motion graphics) more prominent: the centrality of language in these explorations of the

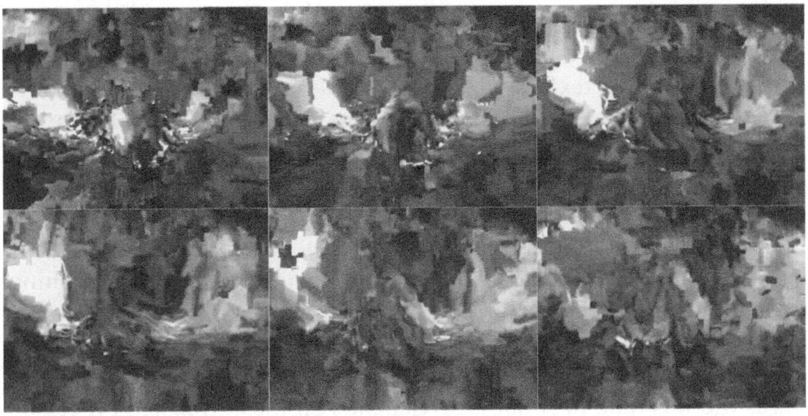

Figure 2.8 Selected stills from *Monster Movie* (2005) by Takeshi Murata

dynamics of words and reading. The fragmentations of *Poemfield No. 2* reveal the continuity between representation, abstract graphics, and typography that form a broad range of expressions dependent on audience recognitions that force a confrontation with the visual process that differentiates between these modes of interpretation (an issue of semiotic engagement). Lexicality reveals itself to be not merely a higher-level erasure of the pictorial, but an additional dimension that parallels these lower-level perceptions, depending on their assignment of domain to *become* language. Both the *Poemfield* films and *Arabesque* demonstrate the importance of *consistent* typography. The fragmentation-repetition of typo/graphy is an accentuation of the inherent organization of type itself: a particular design will contain repetitions of the same letterforms which function as interchangable examples of "type." The issues of selection and combination are fundamental to verbal behavior, a process of *equivalence* expressed in similarity and difference, while their combination proceeds through contiguity.[35] In the *Poemfield* films, as the iterations progress away from their source they become increasingly difficult to recognize as *remaining* typography, an issue for the recognitions of the title cards in *Arabesque* as well. These *graphic expressions* create a visual analogue to Jakobson's semiotic *poetic function*, showing that his proposals for grammatical constructions also apply to typo/graphics and visual poetry generally. As the type's identity disappears, it shifts from *being-language* into *being-image*, a rupture from connotation that returns to denotation. The illusion that words are not indexically informed by the past knowledge and experience of the reader breaks down, forcing the acknowledgement that signification and lexicality impose interpretations that are not innately present 'in' type, form, or image. While the backgrounds in both films originate with typography, not all of these patterns retain a coherent or immediately apparent link with their source text. Binder's *Arabesque* makes these transitions its focus: shots proceed into abstract patterns, erasing the text, while others move back towards *being-typography*, dramatizing these relationships on-screen. In contrast, the *Poemfield* films treat each word/text as a singular, unique moment that repeatedly moves away from language into an all-over composition where the inconsistency of legibility is countered by the consistent linkage of the manipulations to their initial recognition; this knowledge of the lexical form and meaning anchors these shifts into abstraction within the realm of typography.

Typo/graphic interplay between visuality::legibility in the *Poemfield* films (no less than in *Arabesque*) depends on the automated processing and abstraction of the machinic systems that arbitrarily distort the text without concern for its significance or interpretation. This avant-gardist denial of *langue* recurs throughout the twentieth century, a prominent feature of interwar avant-garde movements such as Dada and Surrealism. Belgian typographer Fernand Baudin explains this illustrative role for typo/graphy in his history of its use in both Dada and Surrealist art in the article "Typo-Dada, Dada-Typo." These movements used the graphic potentials of typography to challenge the industrial standardization and common role for writing as a social mechanism of information storage and transfer:

> The subversive scope of Dada is measured in typography as in language. And for good reason. Language, as the foundation of all society, is more important in itself than any philosphical system, than any scale of value. After speech, the most essential expression for the discourse of reason, and of sociality, is writing—in which typography is merely industrial and mechanical reproduction.[36]

Dada forced typography to become a vehicle of expression, through an emphasis on the visuality of the text as both an impediment to legibility and as a source of signification parallel to the words; however, the play of interpretation in these static designs anticipates the dynamics of the 'reading-image,' but can only suggest what motion typography can actually display on-screen. The automated distortions and break-up of language in the commercial title sequences for *Arabesque* or *Doctor Who* belong to this same heritage, more obviously apparent in VanDerBeek and Knowlton's *Poemfield* films; such a link is hardly surprising given the Surrealist influences apparent in VanDerBeek's earlier films, such as *A La Mode* (1957) or *Breathdeath* (1963), which feature metamorphic illusions where multiple images appear one 'inside' another. The Dada and Surrealist engagement with collage poetry is an engagement with the poetic character of typography, a manipulation of language as collage material. The arrangement of lines of cut-out printed text offered a method of engagement with the illustrative possibilities of typography rather than just its lexical functions.

The leader of the Surrealist movement and former Dadaist André Breton's collage poem "Tu seras parmi les victims" ("You will be among the victims," c. 1924), considered as a *typographic* composition, makes this expressive role for the letterforms apparent [Figure 2.9]. The central text of the composition, "On a capté le pollen même des fleurs étranges," offers a graphic suggestion of the

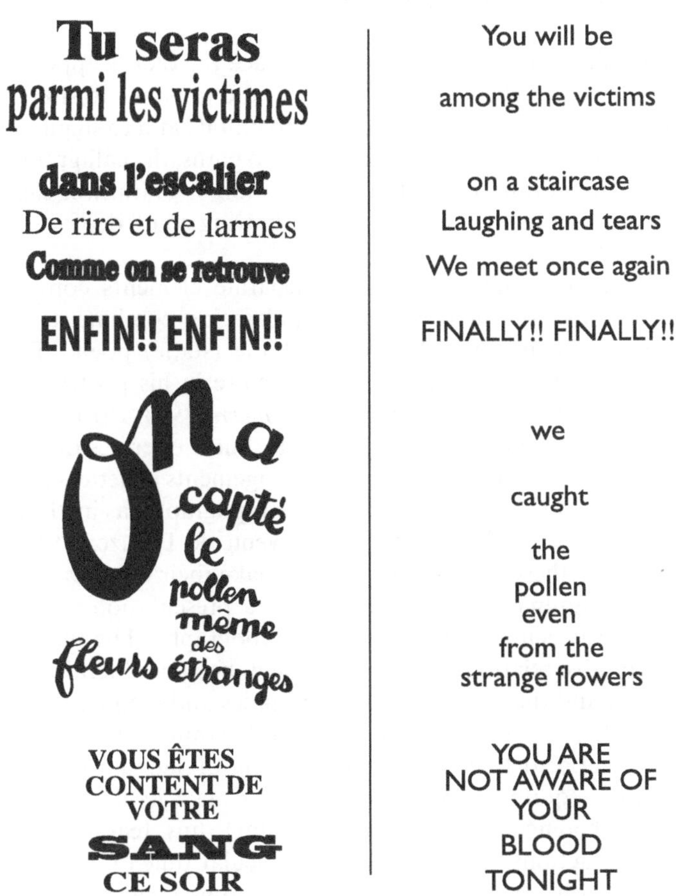

Figure 2.9 "Tu seras parmi les victims" ("You will be among the victims"), Surrealist collage poem by André Breton, c. 1924 [Left: original French text including typeface choices; Right: English translation]

flowers: the open, circular "O" hangs over the rest of this text illustrating the open cone of a flower, while the irregular words form its stem and leaves. The typographic performance depends entirely on the viewer's imagination—their ability to see the flower as a simultaneous affect of the design. This graphic transformation necessitates a (momentary) refusal of the lexical order to apprehend instead another arrangement, one entirely graphic. The recognition of this letterform as simultaneously evoking the form of the "fleurs étranges" requires an abandonment of its lexical significance to understand it as non-language, an inversion of how language dominates those images it accompanies. This ordering role for language-as-vision is revelatory of encultured structures and their essential role in making the world become coherent, as Foucault notes:

> The calligram aspires playfully to efface the oldest oppositions of our alphabetical civilization: to show and to name; to shape and to say; to reproduce and to articulate; to imitate and to signify; to look and to read. Pursuing its quarry by two paths, the calligram sets the most perfect trap. By its double formation, it guarantees capture, as neither discourse alone, nor a pure drawing could do.[37]

In the case of visual poetry, these separate elements converge: the language is also the image; reading and seeing combine as different moments in the process of looking at the (static) poem. The same visuality employed by Guillaume Apollinaire in his poetry collection *Calligrammes: Poèmes de la Paix et de la Guerre, 1913–1916* provides the term of this relationship of text to image, but it operates differently in Breton's poem: Apollinaire's graphic arrangements of letters and words to form images are often hand drawn, *not* typography, as in "Paysage,"[38] or more elaborately in "1915"[39] and "Venu de Dieuze."[40] The static dimensions of these *graphic expressions* make their temporal extension in the 'reading-image' comprehensible as a presentation of the transformation between graphic image and typography. The instability of this interpretive relationship in static design becomes literal as durative progression and the tension between graphics and language in motion. This centrality of an ambivalent visuality illustrates Foucault's concept of power enforced by/through the ordering of language. This power performs (it requires a specific duration to enact its dominance), creating the coherence of the world *as* reading; thus, reading and seeing are different actions, each invoking a particular time of encounter that masks their complex dynamics that are separate conceptual and intellectual engagements.[41] The 'reading-image' in motion design challenges the dominant hierarchy of *reading–seeing–hearing* through reversion and difference, offering a poetic counter-structure whose alterity arises in the changed emphasis and different ordering principles in its construction, a reversal of the typical hierarchy.

The same visuality of letterforms and typo/graphics in *Poemfield No. 2* belongs to this performative engagement, their progression tracing the dissolution of lettering into the background—a reversion to the field—that does not obstruct their meaning. Instead, VanDerBeek's film draws attention to the texts as a 'reading-image' visualizing the communication process, linking his film to the concrete and visual poetry of the 1960s: animated typography and images where lexicality is in flux. Language asserts its dominance over imagery to establish the boundaries of comprehension; however, in these works that relationship reverses this principle of ordering and coherence, drawing attention to the assembly and combination of forms rather than their meaning, offering a different set of limits for interpretive and conceptual possibility than those familiar from everyday communication. This graphic reversal defines the 'reading-image' and provides a link—the *poetic function*—between otherwise distinct avant-garde traditions in motion pictures and (static) visual poetry. The text and titles in these "poemfields" makes this transfer between static visual poetry and the computationally-generated and changed language of motion pictures immanent.

This approach to the *graphic expression* of letterforms in themselves is a common, shared dimension of both graphic design and motion typography. It literally organizes the *kinesis* of 'signage at night' in *N. Y., N. Y.*, the shifting, distorted texts of *Sphere*, as well as the use of graphic, white lines in *The Man With The Golden Arm* that almost immediately became a signifier used in later title sequences to claim the work as "Modern." This quotational design also appears in film title sequences designed by Maurice Binder, and is especially visible in designs made for television programs throughout the 1960s. Its reappearance throughout this period as a graphic quotation-reference signifies the Modernity of the program that follows in ways that are integral to the whole design. These introductory lines only allude to Bass's earlier design; their role is precisely quotational, a statement about a Modernist lineage that is otherwise invisible in the designs shown in Figure 2.10: [row 1] frames from the feature-length documentary film *The James Dean Story* (1958), designed by Maurice Binder; [row 2] frames from *Surprise Package* (1960), using both white and black lines in complementary ways, also designed by Maurice Binder; [row 3] the Freleng–dePatie design for the feature film titles for *The Pink Panther* (1964), showing the play of colored lines; [row 4] the first image of the titles for the television program *The Twilight Zone* (CBS, 1959), showing a doorjamb seen edge-on, spinning in freefall; [row 5] the limited use of title cards in the television program *Boris Karloff's Thriller* (NBC, 1960), entirely composed

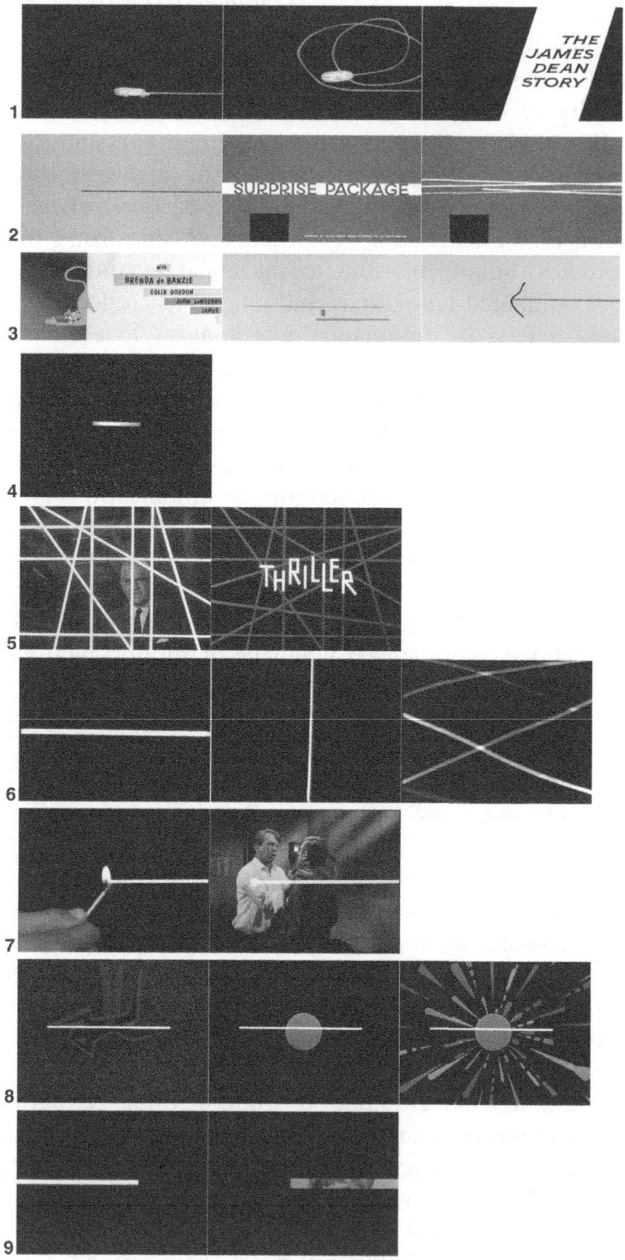

Figure 2.10 Selected stills from film and tv program titles containing white lines: [row 1] *The James Dean Story* (1958); [row 2] *Surprise Package* (1960); [row 3] *The Pink Panther* (1964); [row 4] *The Twilight Zone* (1959); [row 5] *Boris Karloff's Thriller* (1960); [row 6] *The Outer Limits* (1961); [row 7] *Mission Impossible* (1964); [row 8] *Time Tunnel* (1967); [row 9] *The Brady Bunch* (1969)

from a web of individual lines that animate to form the title; [row 6] the first image in the television title sequence for *The Outer Limits* (ABC, 1961), becoming the dynamic waveform pulse of an oscilloscope and reappearing at the conclusion of the sequence; [row 7] the inclusion of the white line is a constant feature throughout the titles for the television program *Mission Impossible* (CBS, 1964), as a burning "fuse" that runs across the entire montage sequence, ending only with the calligram title cards for the case; [row 8] the white lines in *Time Tunnel* (ABC, 1967), which are also integrated with the television title design, providing a visual pause before becoming legible typography; [row 9] the initial introduction of the two parents in *The Brady Bunch* (ABC, 1969) by a white line sliding across the screen before becoming the familiar portrait head arrayed with smaller square portraits for each child. This graphic marker has the same intertextual significance for all these designs in film and television titles. While it does provide a *narrative function* for *Boris Karloff's Thriller* and *Mission Impossible* as an anticipation of the nature of events to follow, for the majority of these designs the presence of the white line is an irrational, but illustrative, excess: it does not relate to the program, its presence instead functioning lexically. In showing the film/television program and its design to be "Modern," this line depends on the same set of learned and internalized referents that define *langue* for semiotics—a set of known, shared referents whose identification is an assignment of meaning. The visuality of this graphic is thus secondary to its legibility as 'white line' in a relationship that inverts the dynamic of images and words (the hierarchy of *reading–seeing–hearing*), undoing their separation through this repeated intertextual quotation.

Using *visuality* to augment and expand the meaning of the text has an extended history in the use of intertitles and other text-on-screen, beginning during the so-called 'silent film' era when the design of title cards also communicated important dimensions of the performance. Designers such as Bob Gill are proponents of this illustrative approach, creating 'skeuomorphic typography': designs where the letterforms and words are also recognizable, pseudo-independent images. Gill uses skeuomorphs to depict the word's meaning—for example, by piling snow on top of the word "ice."[42] The creation of letterforms that are also graphics or which contain pictures is common throughout the history of typography. This use of illustration-figures posed as the letters is a historical aspect of the play of visuality::legibility between images and letterforms,[43] used as a novelty since at least the sixteenth century in pictorial (skeuomorphic) alphabets such as *Der Menschenalphabet* (*The Human Alphabet*, 1534) by Peter Flötner [Figure 2.11]. The selection, arrangement, and resulting typographic composition in Breton's poem uses differences in typeface and weight (regular and bold both appear) to give a graphic emphasis to the other, more standard

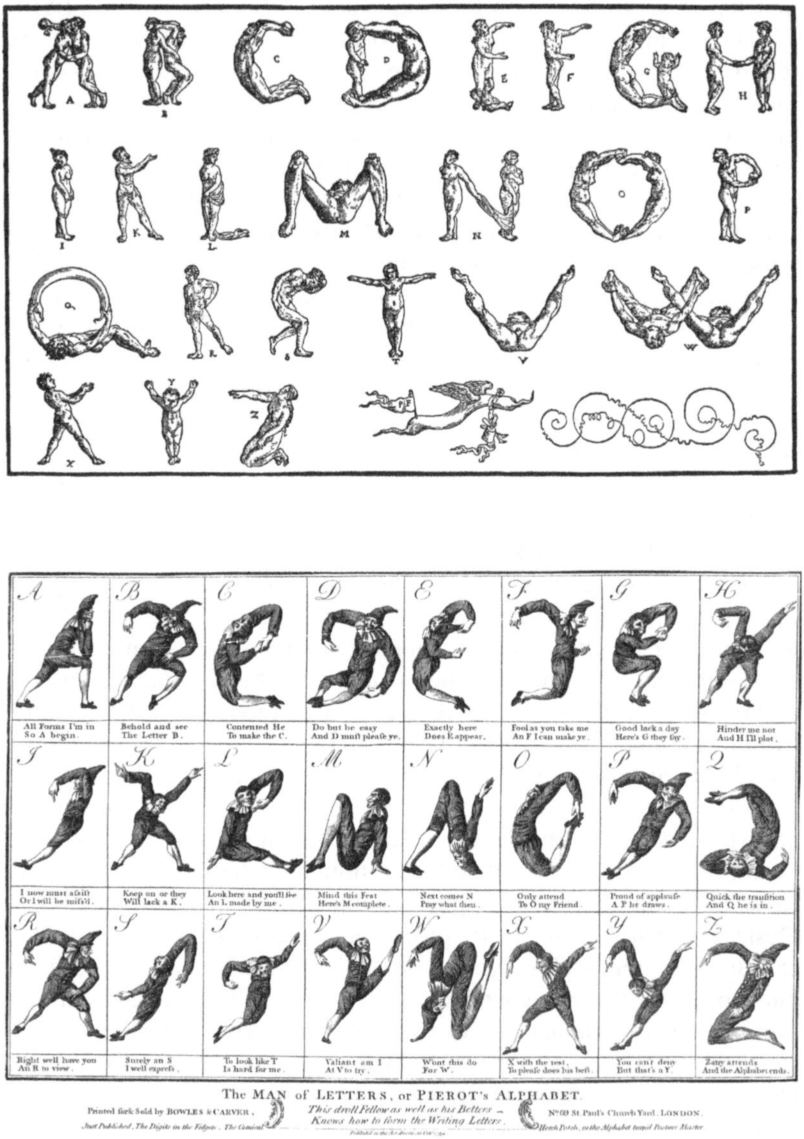

Figure 2.11 Skeuomorphic alphabets: [Top] *Der Menschenalphabet* by Peter Flötner (1534); [Bottom] *The Man of Letters, or Pierrot's Alphabet*, unknown designer, published by Bowles & Carver (1794)

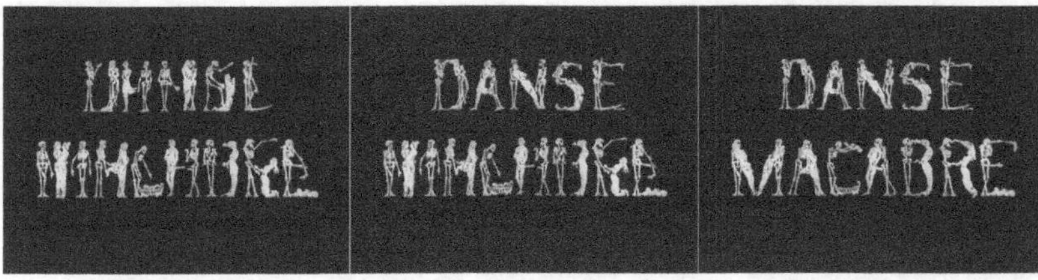

Figure 2.12 Selected stills from the skeuomorphic main title animation in *Danse Macabre* (1921), designed by F. A. A. Dahme

arrangements of words in lines. The animated letterforms appearing in *Danse Macabre* (1921) designed by F. A. A. Dahme [Figure 2.12] uses a combination of deathly skeletons and living humans—mostly women and children—to create a short sequence illustrating the film's name and suggesting its morbid contents. Walter Lantz employs this same skeuomorphic approach in *Abbott and Costello Meet Frankenstein* (1948) for the animated revelation of the main title card from a collection of bones falling into place [Figure 2.13]. Similar transformations of text::image appear in title sequences such as *The Island of Dr. Moreau* (1996), *Flubber* (1997), and *The Mummy* (1999) by designer Kyle Cooper, where graphics imitate typography, or in Will Johnson's title design for *Spring Breakers* (2012), where neon-light graphic images of palm trees and south Floridian kitsch replaces the letterforms. The dynamic interplay between recognizable imagery and the simultaneous, coterminus identification of letterforms and lexicality in these designs offers a visual means to characterize the *nature* of the meaning, even if the text states something banal or ambivalent. These pictorial text-arrangements belong to the tradition of concrete or visual poetry, which has valued the imagistic possibility of type and its arrangement on the page, prioritizing these non-linguistic features as equally important as the legibility of typography. These issues are cyclical, returning to the same dynamics of static designs where the shifting roles of visuality::legibility reveal the distinction that *kinesis* makes for the *graphic expression* on-screen. The transience of engagements that inform the subjective time of reading in graphic design becomes the literal animation process on-screen, giving the performative movements of typo/graphy its significance.

These concerns with visuality and the non-linguistic semiosis of *graphic expressions* are recurring features of the avant-garde's engagement with letterforms and typography. The post-World War II French avant-garde movement Lettrisme is not well known.[44] Being based in

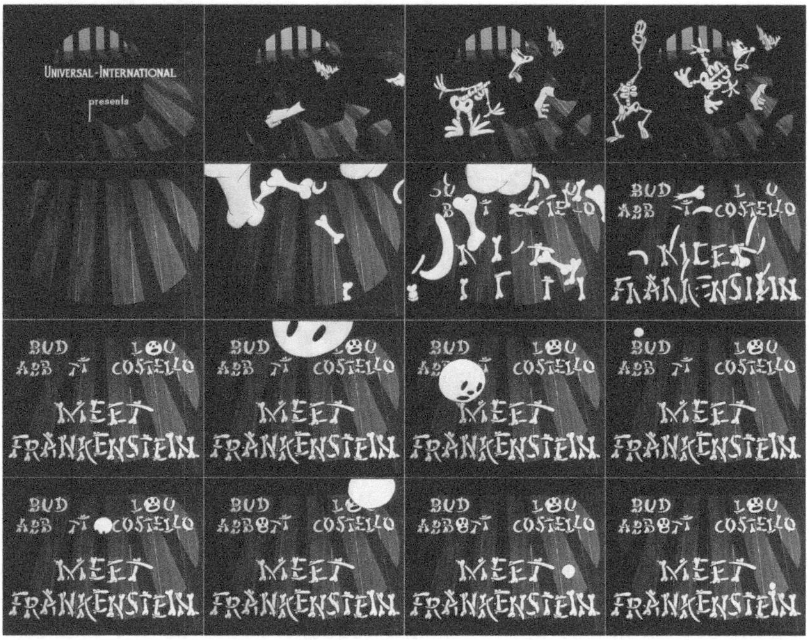

Figure 2.13 Animated title cards from *Abbott and Costello Meet Frankenstein* (1948), designed by Walter Lantz, showing the skeuomorphic main title animation

Paris, this movement was distant to the new art center after the war, New York.[45] The expressive engagement it describes is another, more systematic attempt to develop those potentials employed in Dada and Surrealist works, as Maurice Lemaitre explained in his book *Qu'est-ce que le Lettrisme?* (1954):

> Hypergraphics (formerly metagraphics): ensemble of signs capable of transmitting the reality served by the consciousness more exactly than all the former fragmentary and partial practices (phonetic alphabets, algebra, geometry, painting, music, and so forth).[46]

Lemaitre's description evokes the proposal of Surrealist *automatism* in 1924, but instead of focusing on the subconscious mind and a demonstration of repressed thought,[47] his "Hypergraphics" converge with skeuomorphic typography. Concerns with the arrangement of language and text, especially the capacity of letterforms to become expressive in themselves, creates an atomization of language—*graphic expression*—in

Lettrisme that is typical of concrete poetry generally. It is an engagement with the materiality of written language (an analogue to concerns with verbalization that Jakobson discusses as the *poetic function*) which anticipates the later developments of designers such as David Carson, whose use of vector typefaces laid out on computers in the 1990s also rejected legibility in favor of an expressiveness[48] expanded upon by later developments in both design and art: the rejection of legibility to employ and engage the graphic dimensions of text and language as a material approach to lexicality.[49] These dimensions of visuality are all immanent to the realm of type and its placement on the printed page, but can be translated into motion graphics.

However, the graphic role of text::image is an understanding of the formal issue of legibility that parallels its role in semiotics. Historian-theorist and visual poet Mary Ellen Solt's work with the traditions and complexity of asemiosis in 'visual poetry' is an exploration of relationships between the graphic, skeuomorphic, and typographic identities versus the lexical semiosis of letterforms; their static arrangement on the page anticipates their *kinesis* on-screen in the 'reading-image.' In addition to these considerations of asemic form, visual poets also worked with the graphic dimensions of their text. A consideration of this heritage illuminates the complexities of *graphic expressions*, since they are shared between motion graphics and graphic design. Solt describes her first encounters with these poetic visuals in 1962:

> The Noigandres Group of Brazil [Haroldo de Campos, Augusto de Campos, and Décio Pignatari], who along with Eugene Gomringer of Switzerland founded the international concrete poetry movement, defined the space of the word and by extension the space of the poem as *verbivocovisual* (semantic-aural-visual). This three-dimensional view of the word was realized in poems based on a new concept of form: the **ideogram.** By studying the deployment of words on the page, their visual relationships and juxtapositions, the reader enters into the process of the poem and creates meaning.[50]

The engagement with the visuality of language moves the interpretation from the identification of familiar and known lexical structures into a domain where an interpretive process more common in visual art is employed to derive meaning from the composition and arrangement of letterforms and words—those dimensions of language normally rendered invisible by the process of reading; it is an inversion of the normative engagement where reading dominates sight, allowing the quotations and allusions of visual design to complement and challenge semantic understanding.

The static typography in historical film trailers uses expressive letterforms to communicate the tone, genre, and nature of the movie, an accentuation of the text's lexical content. These promotional exclamations closely resemble static designs—their type does not move, but does involve kinetic wipes and other transitions to provide entrances/exits. The film trailers for both the initial release of *Sh! The Octopus* (1938) and a repertory rerelease of *Dracula* (1951) both employ their texts in the same ways, even though both films are otherwise very different [Figure 2.14]. These superimposed texts behave in similar ways to subtitles—a legible restatement of what the voice-over says—however, their redundancy with the voice-over challenges it for dominance since the graphic aspect communicates more than the spoken words. The transformations of type into visual poetry are an exaggeration of these same material dimensions of typography, pushing towards and past the threshold where the text becomes illegible but retains its identity for the viewer as language. Concrete poetry typically occupies the illegible side of this inflection, while commercial uses of typo/graphics in film trailers and title sequences remains within the realm of recognized, lexical significance.

This engagement with the visual aspects of typo/graphy, paralleling the lexical significance, was a common feature of title designer Kyle Cooper's works in the 1990s. In Andrea Codrington's monograph on Cooper's work, she proposed understanding the role of *graphic expressions* where letterforms and words assume specific roles and disguises which the audience then sees through as a form of typo/graphic performance:

> In many of his title sequences, Cooper creates what could best be described as typographic method acting, wherein words animate in a way that is appropriately symbolic of the film's content.[51]

This conception of "method acting" brings these transformations and shifts in letterform design, legibility, and identity within the scope of familiar narrative constructions, minimizing the challenge their instability poses. The use of familiar symbols from mathematics to replace letters in English in Cooper's design for *Flubber* (1997) [Figure 2.15] neither alters nor challenges their legibility, instead relying on the audience to 'see through' the alterations, understanding them as a playful integration of the credits with the other chemical diagrams appearing on-screen. Similar shifts appear in his design for *The Mummy* (1999) as alternations between hieroglyphics and Latinate lettering, or in the conversion between letters and blood drops for *Dawn of the Dead* (2004). The range of *graphic expressions* employed in these designs always serves as a reiteration of thematics from the narrative itself. The

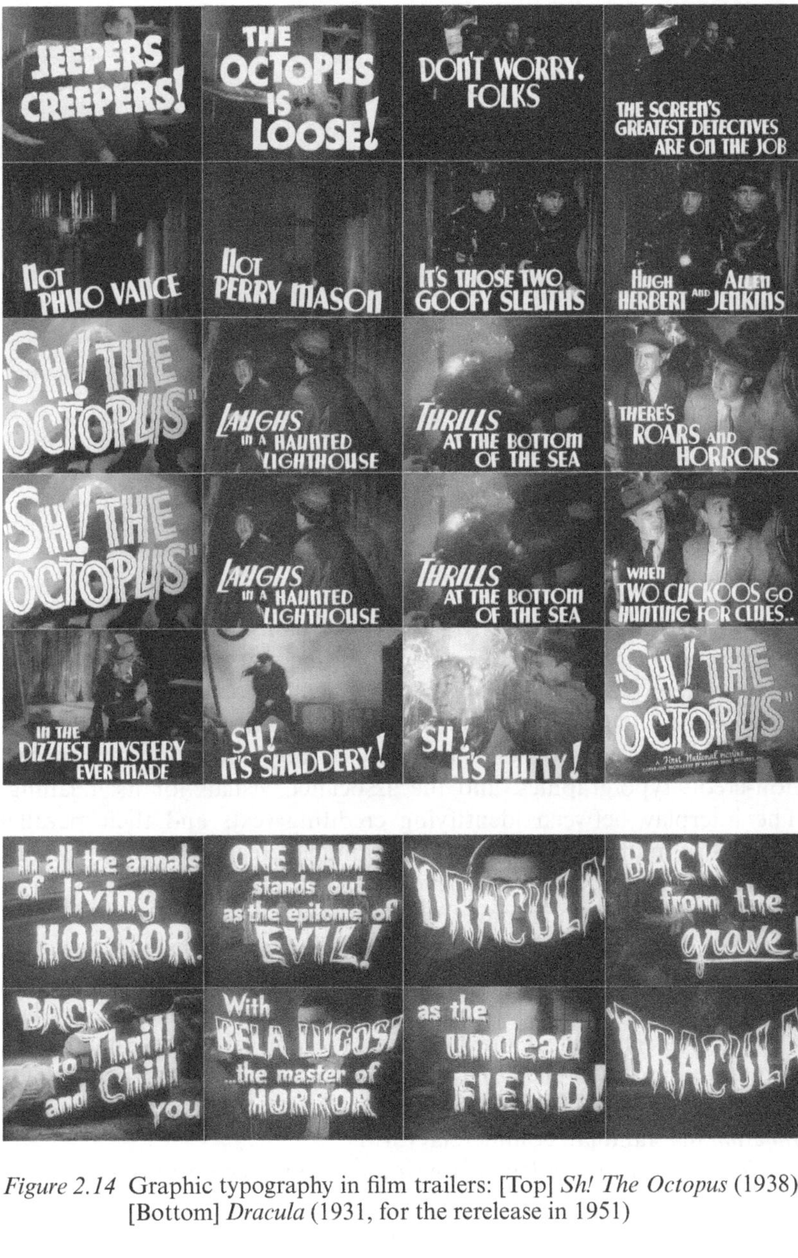

Figure 2.14 Graphic typography in film trailers: [Top] *Sh! The Octopus* (1938); [Bottom] *Dracula* (1931, for the rerelease in 1951)

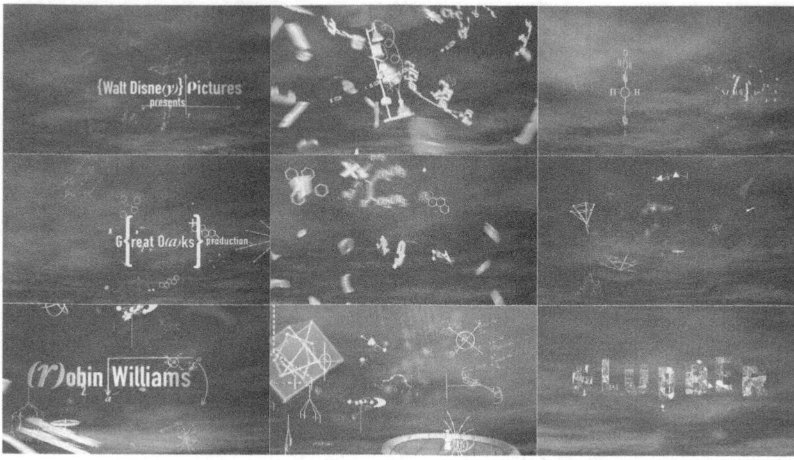

Figure 2.15 Selected stills from the title sequence for *Flubber* (1997), designed by Kyle Cooper

transformation of the non-textual into textuality renders the animated diagrams in *Flubber* as hydrocarbons, graphic plots of tangents, and the cartoonish models of chemistry apparatus all a part of the same visual 'field'—one alluding to a childish view of "doing science." The scientism of this opening depends precisely on the combination of credits, non-credit typo/graphics, and the associated visuals for its meaning. The interplay between identifying crediting texts and their parallel identity as mathematical/scientistic formulae creates a 'reading-image' where both identities are codependent, each emerging from the other as a differential between graphic forms of the symbolic language of mathematics and the letterforms of everyday language: both are instances of language, but they are distinct from one another, separated by meaning and function, even though they share symbols and otherwise overlap. Cooper's designs reflect the heritage of avant-garde experimentation and the visual dynamics of concrete poetry, a commercialization of esoteric and exotic Modernist aesthetics that visually develop the *poetic function* in a familiar, commercial form.

Graphic expressions depend on simultaneous recognitions of graphics in/as letterforms, and the capacity of non-language to behave as language in the indexical links of quotations recognized and understood through past experience. The organization of typo/graphics arises precisely in their overlap and convergence of audience engagements. The ambivalence of perception enables a play of visuality::legibility productive of a specific paralinguistic semiosis where the pictorial informs and changes the meaning of the textual. The soundtrack provides an intermediation in these enunciations, yet the role of sound is always tertiary, dominated by both the visual and textual. Audience interpretations of synchronized sound depends on the syntactic organization provided by their past experiences with audio-visual statements, a set of entangled and overlapping connections that can either reinforce or challenge particular interpretations, but remain supplemental to visuality. The hierarchy of *reading–seeing–hearing* constrains the role of sound. Transformations of meaning erupt suddenly, as a discovery of another level (informed by visual changes or augmented by audible ones), in a recognition of an additional dimension of signification arising from those aspects of reading that are normally ignored and rendered non-signifying: the articulation of forms and their organization on-screen. The issues of morphology and structure are central to the enunciation of graphics apart from the lacunas of type and design.

Notes

1 Golden, W. "Type is to read" *The Visual Craft of William Golden* ed. Cipe Pineles Golden, Kurt Weihs and Robert Stunsky (New York: George Braziller, 1962) pp. 13–35.
2 Stóckl, H. "Typography: body and dress of a text" *Visual Communication 4.2* (June 2005) p. 78.
3 Halas, J. "Visual Revolution" *Film & TV Graphics* (Zurich: The Graphis Press, 1967) pp. 7–18.
4 Schyns, P. G. "Categories and percepts: a bi-directional framework for categorization" *Trends in Cognitive Sciences* vol. 1, no. 5. (August 1997) pp. 183–189.
5 Ziehen, T. *Lehrbuch der Logik auf positivistischer Grundlage mit Berücksichtigung der Geschichte der Logik* (Bonn: A. Marcus & E. Webere Verlag, 1920).
6 Schyns, P. G. "Diagnostic recognition: task constraints, object information and their interactions" *Cognition* 67 (1998) pp. 147–179.
7 Stóckl, H. "Typography: body and dress of a text" *Visual Communication 4.2* (June 2005) p. 78.
8 Foucault, M. *This is not a Pipe* (Berkeley: University of California Press, 1982) pp. 21–25.
9 Baudin, F. "Typo-Dada, Dada-Typo" *Cahiers Dada Surrealism: Dada le la Typography* ed. Fernand Baudin, François Caradec and François Sullerot, vol. 1, no. 3. (1969) pp. 39–41.
10 McMurtrie, D. "The philosophy of Modernism in typography" *Texts on Type* ed. Steven Heller and Phillip Meggs (New York: Allworth Press, 2001) p. 147.
11 Drucker, J. "Graphic Devices: Narration and Navigation" *Narrative* vol. 16, no. 2. (May 2008) pp. 138.
12 Drucker, J. "What is a Word's Body?" *What is? Nine Epistemological Essays* (Victoria: Cuneform Press, 2013) p. 38.

13 Drucker, J. "What is a Word's Body?" *What is? Nine Epistemological Essays* (Berkeley: Cuneiform Press, 2013) pp. 33–45.
14 Tyler, P. *The Underground Film: A Critical History* (New York: Grove Press, 1968) pp. 143.
15 Shaviro, S. *Post Cinematic Affect* (Washington: Zero Books, 2010) pp. 11–12.
16 Shaviro, S. *Post Cinematic Affect* (Washington: Zero Books, 2010) pp. 11–12.
17 Quist, A. "Developing Expressive Animorphs" *Animation: An Interdisciplinary Journal* vol. 12, no. 1. (2017) pp. 7–27.
18 Quist, A. "Developing Expressive Animorphs" *Animation: An Interdisciplinary Journal* vol. 12, no. 1. (2017) pp. 7–27.
19 Jakobson, R. *Selected Writings III: Poetry of Grammar and Grammar of Poetry* (New York: Mouton Publishers, 1981) p. 25.
20 Jakobson, R. *Selected Writings III: Poetry of Grammar and Grammar of Poetry* (New York: Mouton Publishers, 1981) p. 22.
21 Federici, F. "Is asemic writing a zero-point writing? (Asemic Draft in progress n.3)" *Utsanga.it* no. 15. (March 2018) ed. Francesco Aprile and Cristiano Caggiula utsanga.it/federici-is-asemic-writing-zero-point-writing/ March 27, 2018, retrieved April 10, 2018
22 Johnson, C. B. *Modernity Without a Project* (Brooklyn: Punctum Books, 2015).
23 Drucker, J. "Who's Afraid of Visual Culture" *Art Journal* vol. 58, no. 4. (Winter 1999) pp. 37.
24 Betancourt, M. *The History of Motion Graphics: From Avant-Garde to Industry in the United States* (Holicong: Wildside Press, 2013) pp. 210–222.
25 Armitage, M. "Movie Titles" *Print* vol. 5, no. 2. (February 1, 1947) p. 45.
26 MacDonald, S. *Art in Cinema* (Philadelphia: Temple University Press, 2006) p. 3.
27 Richter, H. "The Film as an Original Art Form" in *College Art Journal* vol. 10, no. 2. (Winter 1951), pp. 157–161.
28 Betancourt, M. *Semiotics and Title Sequences: Text–Image Composites in Motion Graphics* (New York: Routledge Focus, 2017) pp. 75–91.
29 Drucker, J. *What is? Nine Epistemological Essays* (Berkeley: Cuneiform Press, 2013) p. 59.
30 Foucault, M. *This is not a Pipe* (Berkeley: University of California Press, 1983) p. 24.
31 Palmer, B. *Ben at the Beeb: Recollections of a life in the BBC by Ben Palmer, 1947–1983* (spiral bound typescript, revised February 2005) pp. 67–68.
32 Sutton, G. *The Experience Machine* (Cambridge: The MIT Press, 2015) pp. 162–164.
33 Foucault, M. *The Order of Things* (New York: Pantheon, 1970) p. 48.
34 Betancourt, M. "Glitched Media as Found/Transformed Footage: Post-Digitality in Takeshi Murata's *Monster Movie* (2005)" *Found Footage Magazine* no. 3. (March 2017) pp. 48–57.
35 Jakobson, R. *Selected Writings III: Poetry of Grammar and Grammar of Poetry* (New York: Mouton Publishers, 1981) p. 27.
36 Baudin, F. "Typo-Dada, Dada-Typo" *Cahiers Dada Surrealism: Dada le la Typography* ed. Fernand Baudin, François Caradec and François Sullerot, vol. 1, no. 3. (1969) p. 41.

37 Foucault, M. *This is not a Pipe* (Berkeley: University of California Press, 1982) pp. 20–22.
38 Apollinaire, G. *Calligrammes: Poèmes de la Paix et de la Guerre, 1913–1916* (Paris: Libraire Gallimard, 1925) p. 18.
39 Apollinaire, G. *Calligrammes: Poèmes de la Paix et de la Guerre, 1913–1916* (Paris: Libraire Gallimard, 1925) p. 92.
40 Apollinaire, G. *Calligrammes: Poèmes de la Paix et de la Guerre, 1913–1916* (Paris: Libraire Gallimard, 1925) pp. 118–119.
41 Foucault, M. *This is not a Pipe* (Berkeley: University of California Press, 1982) p. 25.
42 Gill, B. "Words Into Pictures" (Mulgrave: Images Publishing, 2009) p. 10.
43 Gill, B. "Words Into Pictures" (Mulgrave: Images Publishing, 2009) pp. 6–7.
44 Seaman, D. "Lettrisme—A Stream that Runs Its Own Course" *Visible Language (Lettrisme: Into The Present)* special issue ed. Stephen C. Foster, vol. 17, no. 3. (1983) pp. 18–25.
45 Cohen-Solal, A. *Painting American* (New York: Knopf, 2001).
46 Lemaitre, M. *Qu'est-ce que le Lettrisme?* quoted in Foster, S. "Lettrisme: A Point of Views" *Visible Language (Lettrisme: Into The Present)* special issue ed. Stephen C. Foster, vol. 17, no. 3. (1983) p. 7.
47 Breton, A. *Manifestoes of Surrealism* trans. Richard Seaver and Helen R. Lane (Ann Arbor: Ann Arbor Paperbacks, 1972) pp. 24–26.
48 Blackwell, L. *The End of Print: The Graphic Design of David Carson* (San Francisco: Chronicle Books, 1995) pp. 14–20.
49 Curtay, J-P. "Super-Writing 1983—American 1683" *Visible Language (Lettrisme: Into The Present)* special issue ed. Stephen C. Foster, vol. 17, no. 3. (1983) pp. 26–56.
50 Solt, M. E. "Words and Spaces (c. 1985)" *OEI no, 51: Toward a Theory of Concrete Poetry* special issue ed. Antonio Sergio Bessa, no. 51. (2010) p. 3.
51 Codrington, A. *Kyle Cooper* (New Haven: Yale Monographics, 2003) p. 15.

3 Chronic Progression

Typography involves a modal distinction between immanence and emergence. Both the self-contained (momentary) nature of *kinetic action*, and the immanent, formal appearance of letterforms and other marks in *graphic expression* involve an immediate, proximate engagement, while the organization of *chronic progression* in the 'reading-image' is specifically and precisely apparent as the emergent apprehension of the *kinesis* for the type-as-a-whole. The *chronic* is a constant process happening over literal time, *durational*, that tends to be invisible, ignored in analysis as a redundant feature of articulation. This mode becomes apparent from its role in specific, liminal situations where the legibility *of* text, and its identification *as* text happen as separate recognitions by the audience—a *holistic* progression that includes all the transitional entrances and exits, forming and unforming of the letterforms. The significance of the TV station logo ident made by Scanimate for the WTOP-TV station in Washington, DC in 1975 [Figure 3.1] emerges from its continuous transformation of the unspooling and illegible "9," indicating that the station has *dynamic* programming. The sequence of transformative distortions in this nine-second long ident for the TV station employs a morphing of the number "9" as its dominant visual, appearing on-screen for four seconds by itself. The progression from illegibility into legibility matches the duration of this animation precisely; it is a *graphic expression* within the larger *chronic progression* of this 'reading-image.' The spinning text of "WTOP-TV" enters three seconds into this transformation. Neither text is initially legible, yet their identity as lexical forms is never in doubt. In recognizing this short animation as a logo presentation—apparent from the first frame with its graphic pattern of spinning dots—the audience anticipates that the text will become legible, understands that what they are seeing is going to become typography. The rapid progression from graphic pattern to legibility happens within the first four seconds, meeting this expectation almost immediately. The number is fully legible for the second half of the animation; both additional texts, stating "Washington, DC" and "WTOP-TV," are instances

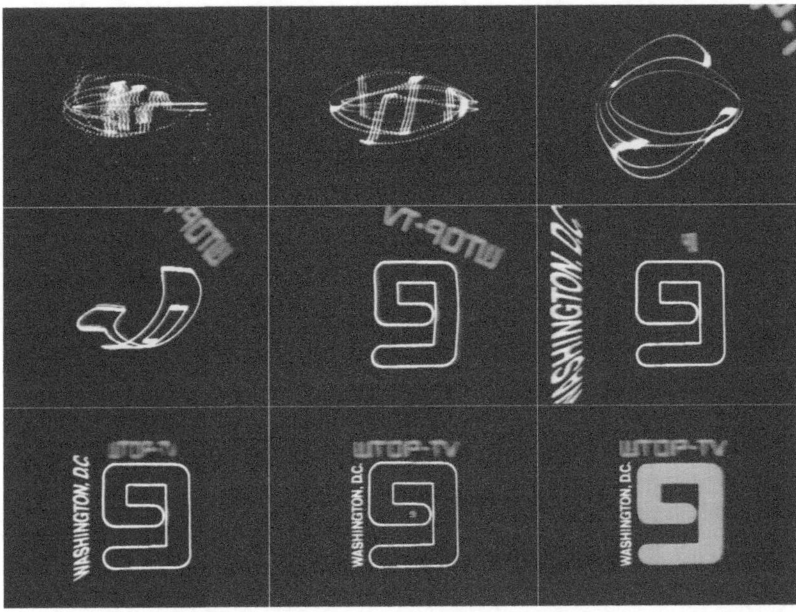

Figure 3.1 Stills showing the text transformations in the logo resolve ident for WTOP-TV, Washington, DC, produced by Scanimate (1975)

of what Brownie terms "scrolling layout,"[1] where the blocks of text move as recognizable and legible units. The approximately five seconds that these three texts are all on-screen together and fully legible gives the viewer an opportunity to read them while appreciating the dynamic presentation used to move these elements into place. The filling-in of the number at the conclusion serves to unify the design (all the text is a solid color) as a singular graphic unit, concluding the animation and the logo ident sequence. The synchronized music matches the motion and provides a crescendo as the "9" is filled in. The emergence of this number makes the relationship of *chronic progression* and the issues of legibility apparent.

A similar 'reading-image' whose *chronic progression* includes briefer *kinetic actions* appears in Peter Frankfurt's design for *The Number 23* (2007). A large, emergent "23" composed from the individually typed "23"s that surround and contain the other credits and typography is revealed at the conclusion of the title sequence as a dark red liquid (blood?) that has soaked the page, finally covering it entirely. This steady emergence of the large "23" unifies the credits throughout the sequence, its eventual full revelation coming after a series of partial and suggestive

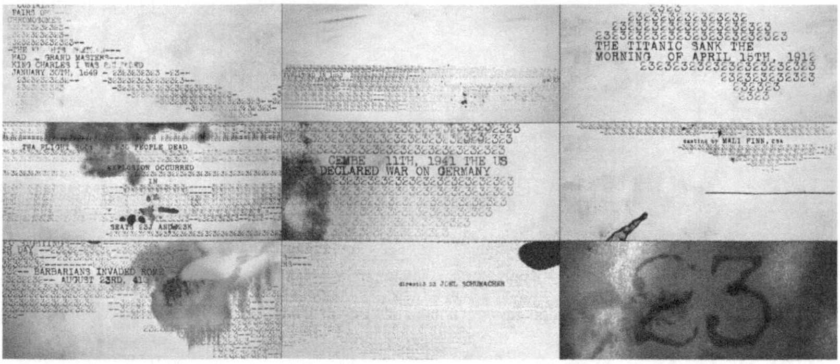

Figure 3.2 Selected stills from the title sequence for *The Number 23* (2007), designed by Peter Frankfurt, showing the emergent "23"

'asemic' shots that contain pieces of this larger text [Figure 3.2] without verifying its identity as *text*. Progression into legibility makes the analysis and consideration of asemic typography essential to the modal comprehension of *chronic progression*, offering an opportunity to consider *duration* as a revelatory process. Motion demands a consideration not only of text-on-screen as an immanent, *animated* expression, but of its appearance over time in an emergent, graphic progression, a question betraying the importance of *chronological* arrangement to interpretation. This *kinesis* demonstrates that comprehending motion typography relies on its temporal organization emerging over time, and intersects with the audience's lexical expertise gained from past experiences.

The centrality of audience engagement distinguishes the visual encounter from its transformation in/through written language—typography began as the pictograph, the hieroglyph, the icon. Recognizing visual imagery as *lexical* requires a transformation of image into verbal language that is a fundamental shift in comprehension and engagement. These higher-level engagements with visuality are guided by the expectation that the immanent encounter is (or will become) meaningful when engaged with the appropriate indexical expertise, shifting interpretation towards what philosopher Martin Heidegger has called "curiosity":

> When curiosity has become free, it takes care to see not in order to understand what it sees, that is, to come to a being toward it, but *only* in order to see. It seeks novelty only to leap from it again to another novelty. The care of seeing is not concerned with comprehending and knowingly being in the truth, but with possibilities of abandoning itself to the world.[2]

"Curiosity" approaches textuality via its *asemic* dimensions, apart from their signification and lexical indexicality, challenging Foucault's hierarchy of *reading–seeing–hearing* for dominance by undermining the difference between *denotation* (visuality) and *connotation* (lexicality). The 'reading-image' engages these dynamics to consider typography without eliding the visual to engage its meaning 'transparently'—the typical seeing-through-visuality that is *reading.* Heideggerian "curiosity" is an active viewership that engages in the world as an experience where comprehension (in the linguistic sense of lexical order and its prioritization of textual significance) becomes secondary to that encounter. Asemic typography confounds these 'transparent' distinctions between denotation and connotation, returning the separation of perception and thought normally erased by the lexical identification. As meaning reverts into form, the connotations associated with semiosis become instead the denotation "letterforms" (without attached signification) in a reversal of lexicality, since normally *only* connotation transforms the visual into an expression of thought. These dynamics play out in immanent recognitions apparent when viewing static designs of visual (concrete) poetry that employ asemic forms as a revelation of familiar interpretive processes and lexical structures, but without typical semiotic engagements [Figure 3.3]. Motion typography generally restricts this asemic character because *kinesis* does not limit the design to a singular arrangement on-screen; however, the tension around legibility and lexicality is not diminished by these differences.

Motion undermines typography's foundations in the static compositions of graphic design that are productive of 'asemic' text. The two formal organizations Barbara Brownie proposes in her book on motion typography both rely on *kinesis* for their definition: "dynamic layout" and "scrolling layout." These layout types move typography as unitary blocks (scrolling layout), or move and rearrange a more fragmentary typography—ranging from individual strokes to letters and words—as *independent* animated units (dynamic layout). The potential for motion typography to engage in the play of Heideggerian "curiosity" is attenuated by designs where the typography only undergoes slight transformation, but this capacity for visualizing the recognition and interpretive process in the emergent form of the type (*chronic progression*) remains constant in both categories Brownie proposes. While these two methods of organization are employed throughout the history of motion typography, "dynamic layout" has become more common with the ease of production offered by digital computers, while "scrolling layout" is a common feature of older designs produced by hand, suggesting the significance of automated computer technology for increased movement on-screen. Brownie uses the proposition of asemic

Figure 3.3 Asemic composition, *2013_010 July 17, 2013* by Michael Betancourt/ Artists Rights Society

typography to separate motion typography from static type designs; the historical shift from one production technology to another creates barriers to the conceptualization of what can and might be possible for the 'reading-image' in motion graphics because of an assumed overlap with graphic design. Her concerns in asemic typography are with the ambivalence created by motion typography that results in its illegibility, and thus lexical unintelligibility:

> In challenging the reader to read something that he or she cannot, asemisis reduces the reader to a state of feeling uninformed or uneducated. The asemic signs in Xu Bing's *Book From Sky* relate to issues of cultural misunderstanding and miscommunication, specifically the sense of discomfort that may be experienced when one is faced with signs that cannot be deciphered.[3]

Brownie's assumption that foreign languages are a cause of discomfort is itself problematic. Her claim that unknown language leads to a feeling of being "uninformed or uneducated" is presumptuous, even colonial. There are many languages in the world, so to assume that encountering an unknown language would result in the viewer feeling "uninformed or uneducated" makes the assumption that they *should* know every language, that encountering a foreign language is a demeaning and disenfranchising experience—a peculiar and irrelevant claim for a discussion of typography. An unknown language is simply that: unknown. What is important in her discussion is the recognition that *when* a viewer understands and identifies the material encountered as *lexical*—as having a meaning, even if that meaning remains unknown—it *cannot* be "asemic" even if the viewer lacks the expertise to interpret the meaning: untranslatable and unknown is *not* the same as meaningless.

Uncertainty and ambivalence define asemic typography. Our engagement with it leaves us conscious of the unfamiliarity (but not uncanniness) of lexical forms we do not understand. It is an epistemological uncertainty that originates with a failure to produce familiar resolutions of meaning in semiosis: we cannot read these works, instead we *see* them, and our engagement is forced to proceed through the visual (not textual) dimensions of our encounter. The problematic of how lexical expertise leads to recognitions of semiotic structures in works where there is no familiar semiotic structure—the foundational state for 'asemic' and 'concrete' or visual poetry—is a focus of critical concern for those visual poets explicitly engaged with the materiality of writing, such as Federico Federici, who noted these problems of lexicality for the asemic:

> Asemic texts seem to constantly rely on the reader's canny clairvoyance to disclose their meaning, not to leave him standing before the

> melancholic contemplation of its loss. For this reason, they may appear as a radical, conceptual research into the nature of language, which intentionally drops the contents of experience and hides behind the mimicry of well known languages. [...] In asemic scripts, on the contrary, signs and meanings have been superseded by the pure notion of *asemicism*, wherein the writing itself becomes a delay in meaning.[4]

The centrality of recognizing lexical potential as foundational for reading cannot be underestimated. These works remind us that perception is not a matter of lexical semiosis—our ability to explain and interpret through language comes after the initial visual moment. The issues Federici identifies for asemic poetry lies not with its being *unintelligible*, but with the ways that it invokes the conventional understanding of lexicality, of belonging to *langue* (governed by the system of abstract language rules) but without coherent *parole* (a meaning-creating statement produced by those rules). The *asemic* is an inversion of the classic relations of semiosis: the evidence of linguistic form apparent in asemic poetry does not result in a legible statement or a specific meaning. Instead, these works direct attention to the boundary between coherence and incoherence, making the role of encultured articulation that organizes enunciation apparent.

Asemic compositions confront a failing that Heidegger noted about our encounters—that our attempts to interpret the world around us assume that we can be certain about those encounters. Understanding their dynamics as static compositions informs the differences presented by *kinesis*: these texts inaugurate an epistemological regression into uncertainty that originates with a failure of semiosis. We cannot *read* the asemic; instead we look, and our attempt to read is forced to proceed through a visual engagement with denotation, evoking text rather than connotation. The active shift that returns to seeing from reading is *and* is not an experience from our everyday lives. The attention to the process of interpretation that is arrested by/in asemic poetry makes the commonplace 'transparency' of engagement into an 'opacity' Heidegger addresses:

> Here being-in-the-world is from the very beginning geared towards interpreting, opining, being certain, and having faith, a kind of behavior which is in itself always already a founded mode of being-in-the-world.[5]

Asemic typography draws attention to the artifice of apparently stable interpretations: once these visual forms have been identified *as* language, the viewer always engages these materials with an expectation of meaning that structures and directs their apprehension of the morphologies on view; this factor remains true for motion typography as well. Asemic poetry shifts the interpretive engagement from the 'transparency' of seeing-through visuality to engage in semiosis with those dimensions of form that make *lexical* semiosis possible. This shift from meaning conveyed through signs (connotation) to an emphasis on visual elaboration of meaning through the other aspects of text and typography makes the *visual* dimensions (denotation) of the 'text' dominant. Instead of a concern with lexical meanings known through past experience, the shift in priorities of interpretation that Frederici describes is a change from reading to the visuality of texts as the primary means of their enunciation. The *asemic* emphasizes the formal elements of typography that the introduction to Ellen Lupton and Abbott Miller's *Design Writing Research: Writing on Graphic Design* identifies as the differential between material presentation (denotation) and meaning (connotation):

> Spacing and punctuation, borders and frames: these are the territory of typography and graphic design, those marginal arts that render texts and images readable. The substance of typography lies not in the alphabet as such—the generic forms of characters and their conventional uses—but rather in the framework and specific graphic forms that materialize the system of writing. Design and typography work at the *edges* of writing, determining the shape and style of letters, the spaces between them, and their placement on the page. Typography, from its position at the margins of communication, has moved writing away from speech.[6]

As writing moves verbal communication away from speech, typography also moves it away from the drawn, graphic image. Concern with *asemic* dimensions is a concern with the "edges" of text and language, where the visual appearance of the text becomes a signifier in itself. For motion typography, *kinesis* performs this action: the motion of the letters/words, the dynamic composition on-screen, and the development of that work expressed via *chronic progression* marks the temporal elaboration of typography from the beginnings of its appearance on-screen until it exits as a singular expressive unit. *Kinesis* distinguishes the role of 'asemic' motion-forms, allowing their arrangement and progression to transition *between* being recognized and being legible—identifying the presence of text-on-screen is not the same as being able to understand what that text states, nor is legibility the same as lexical comprehension, as when an audience is confronted by text in an unfamiliar language. The 'reading-image' describes this literal time (duration) for recognition-interpretation where the audience makes the category assignment of *language* as a separate phenomenon from understanding its semiosis.

The undercurrents of legibility, lexicality, and familiarity have specific roles within visual and asemic poetry that also apply to motion typography: these dimensions have a long history in static typography, extending throughout the avant-garde works of the twentieth century and into the deeper past. Avant-garde typographer and artist Kurt Schwitters's *Merz* poem "Ursonate," composed from 1922–1932, applies the musical sonata form to the arrangement and sequencing of 'nonsense' words and noises whose organization evokes language without producing a specific linguistic meaning.[7] This poem was animated in Ed Ackerman's film *Primiti Too Taa* (1988) as typewriting gliding around the screen [Figure 3.4]. Explicitly employing unknown but word-like compositions whose declamatory presentation in the voice-over synchronized with their animation renders these 'nonsense' words simultaneously comprehensible and unfamiliar—they withhold a recognized lexical meaning while evoking known significations in the familiar enunciative forms of questions, exclamations, and declarations. However, the composition is undoubtedly *asemic*: the audience is unable to connect

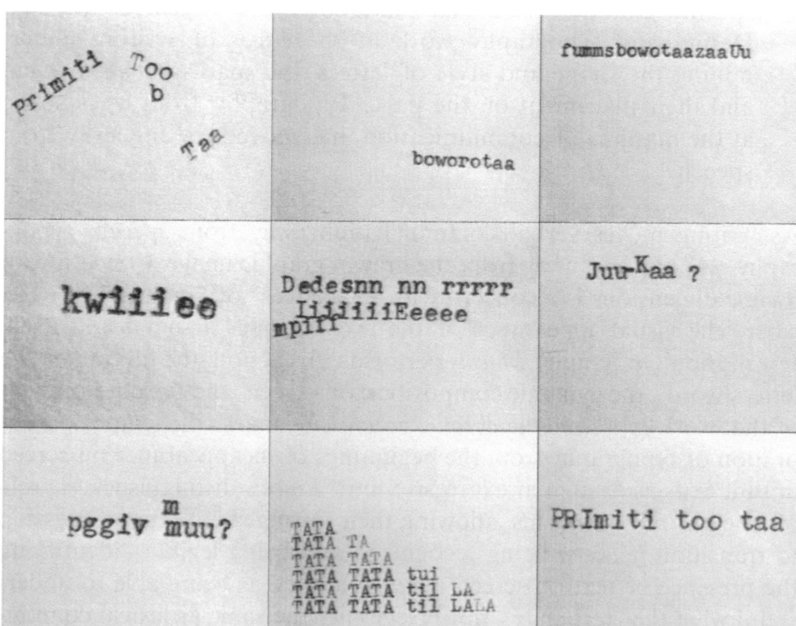

Figure 3.4 Selected stills from *Primiti Too Taa* (1988) by Ed Ackerman

known (established) meanings for the words shown to their lexical structure. This divergence from familiarity does not mean the audience is unable to interpret any meaning, nor that they feel uneducated (as Brownie claims). The Latin alphabet is employed throughout *Primiti Too Taa*. Verbal sounds synchronized with the text (words and letters) correspond to their familiar pronunciations, but without the typical relationship to known language. The result is defamiliarized (unknown words) organized to form familiar letter/sound relationships. Instead of being entirely unknown, the results are simultaneously familiar and unknown, but *not* alienating. An estrangement of sounds from familiar language is countered by the known, established relationships of letter/sound combinations. While the audience does not know the language being presented, neither Schwitters's "Ursonate" nor Ackerman's *Primiti Too Taa* undermines their established knowledge and expertise with lexical relationships in the way that a different letter/sound combination than what is normally used would. In listening/watching *Primiti Too Taa*, its lexical nature is obvious and the familiarity of letter/sound combinations combine to present recognizable meanings through the verbal, onomatopoetic performance that renders the text visibly comprehensible through *kinesis* as, for example, in the swirling collection of "e"s that fills the screen, only the be 'blown away' by the abrupt "bo" [Figure 3.5].

Although composed from 'nonsense,' the use of familiar text::sound combinations serves an essential function in explaining the rest of the unknown text in the film: it becomes a performance of phoneme-sounds and animated typewriting that uses the established knowledge and expectations for letter/sound relationships to explore their 'free play' without the familiar and regimented function 'speech.' This distinction decouples verbalization and typography from their communicative functions *qua* language, but does not render the results meaningless except as lexical signs: they become signifiers for a fugitive graphic and expressive *parole* that simultaneously invokes and denies *langue*, opening a chasm between them.

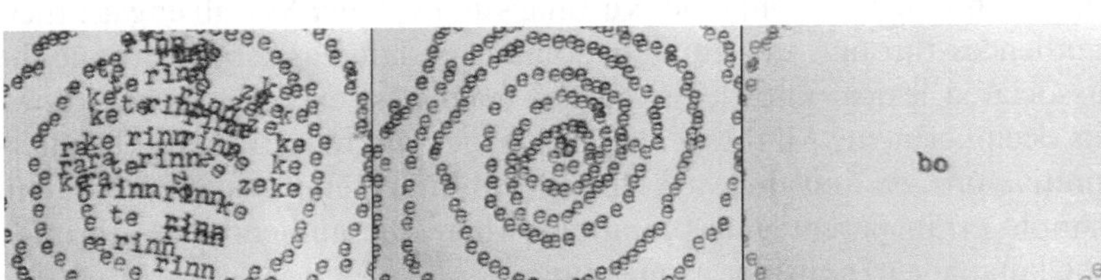

Figure 3.5 Selected stills from *Primiti Too Taa* (1988) by Ed Ackerman, showing onomatopoetic typography

Passages of performative, animated text in *Primiti Too Taa* converge on a singular meaning that is *not* linguistic, revealing the density of semic and asemic typography. The lexical content of the text animated and arranged on-screen remains entirely unknown—*asemic*—yet this film does not create a sense of dismay, as Brownie's discussion suggests; in fact, quite the opposite. It draws attention to the role of the audience in rendering-coherent what appears to be meaningless. Roland Barthes's discussion of the issues of denotation, connotation, and all their entangled complexities in painting also describes their relations for asemic texts where changes in perception become shifts in comprehension:

> It is by an effort of distance, by changing the level of perception, that I receive another message, a hyper-metropic apparatus which, like a decoding grid, allows me suddenly to perceive the total meaning, the "real" meaning. [...] Distance and proximity are promoters of meaning. Everything proceeds from spacing out or staggering of articulations.[8]

The conscious choice of the observer in *how* to look is the source of meaning in works where the ambivalence of appearance becomes a reflection on the interpretive process rendered as the content of the encounter with asemic poetry. The interplay of voice-over and synchronized motion typography mediates the defamiliarization in *Primiti Too Taa*: the interaction between letterforms, unknown words, and familiar pronunciations elides these texts' foreignness. Although the words are 'nonsense,' their formal presentation corresponds to the familiar structure and organization of Indo-European languages: the syllables and declarative presentation remain within the scope of expectation for those languages, rendering their signification apparent by invoking *langue* without the explicit communication of *parole.* The enjoyment of asemic text in *Primiti Too Taa* lies precisely with how it is made from 'nonsense' that evokes familiar lexical associations without delivering a lexical meaning; it is a 'playing' with perception and interpretation that Heideggerian "curiosity" actively describes. Ackermann's film, Schwitters's poem, and Xu Bing's *Book From Sky* all engage their audiences through the familiar domain of language, but without the associated lexical knowledge gained from past experience that allows its decipherment. All these 'reading-images' are reflections on the interpretive process and the ways that lexical interpretations are more than simple, 'transparent' interpretations where the audience sees through the language to consider its meaning.

The organization of lexical forms offers familiar modes of engagement that impose a structure on how their audience renders the arrangement of elements as *potentially informational.* Parsing material elements (letters, sounds) into groupings to create articulations, these arrangements are then compared to past experience and established lexical expertise; if they are familiar from past experience, this activity renders them meaningful. The particular significance for any enunciation *only* comes at the conclusion of this process, as a third moment in this series of actions. Asemic texts separate the final, interpretive moment from the earlier activities that led to it, allowing a consideration of the formative processes of articulation and enunciation that behave like a "bucket-brigade," where earlier decisions carry forward to influence and shape later choices.[9] These discrete activities, each a particular stage in a series, illuminate Brownie's theorization of the asemic elements of motion typography: the recognition of meaning depends first on its identification as being linguistic, but once a visual form has that category assignment, its understanding proceeds explicitly as a function of semiotics: the isolation and separation of the letterforms and their familiar groupings to form words on-screen, as in a title sequence, is a fusion of concerns with legibility, design aesthetics, and animation that mirror what Michael Foucault describes in *The Archaeology of Knowledge.* These dynamics arise from the audience's recognition that a set of visuals corresponds to lexical form:

> The statement is neither a syntagma, nor a rule of construction, nor a canonic form of succession and permutation; it is that which enables such groups of signs to exist, and enables these rules or forms to become manifest. But although it enables them to exist, it does so in a special way—a way that must not be confused with the existence of signs as elements of a language (*langue*), or with the material existence of those marks that occupy a fragment of space or last for a variable length of time.[10]

This process of expectation organizing and guiding interpretation is apparent in the animated title card for J. Stuart Blackton's cartoon *Humorous Phases of Funny Faces* (1906), in which the title forms from a series of fragmentary strokes whose arrangement and accumulation becomes the letterforms of the title [Figure 3.6]. Audience expectations for lexical organization governs the apprehension of all these elements as they appear one by one: the enunciation created in an array of marks becomes an apparent *statement* before it becomes meaningful as language. The addition of animation and the temporal development it always implies is transformative of historical constraints on legibility. Because the material existence of those marks that form the typography of the title have an identical size, and are arranged into clear rows spaced evenly across the screen, their identification as *writing* is almost immediate, even though the precise words being shown are not instantly

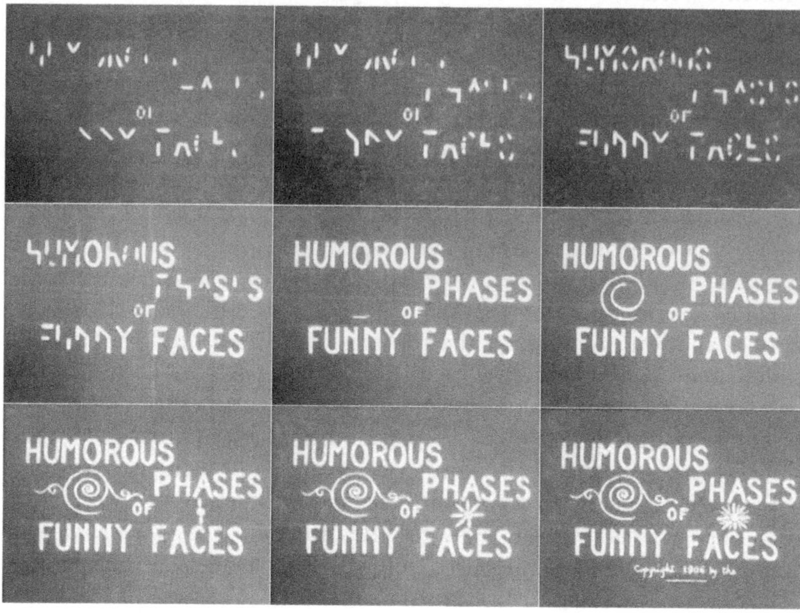

Figure 3.6 All the title cards in *Humorous Phases of Funny Faces* (1906) by J. Stuart Blackton

apparent. This process of audience adaptation to the conditions of the work is an interpretive act that understands the text-on-screen 'transparently,' focusing on its meaning rather than its material organization: the text becomes *fully* comprehensible *before* the letterforms are completely formed, a demonstration of the audience's past experience recognizing the partial words on-screen and completing the text in advance. The audience's *active* engagement with what they encounter is a process of decipherment, but one where their activity is primarily fixed upon the enunciations and order arising from accepting its articulation.

Richard Greenberg's two-minute title sequence design for the science-fiction film *Alien* (1979) [Figure 3.7] converges on the same recognition of the fragmentation and revelation of language from constituent marks apparent in the 20-second long title for *Humorous Phases of Funny Faces* (1906). Unlike Blackton's design, where the distinction between fragmented letterforms and animated drawings creates a hieratic distinction between elements, the arrangement of text-on-screen in *Alien* renders the hierarchy a literal feature of the design: asemic lines that *will* form the word "ALIEN" are placed directly at the top of the screen, their progression towards coherent legibility contrasting with the legible credits *for* the production appearing centrally below. These

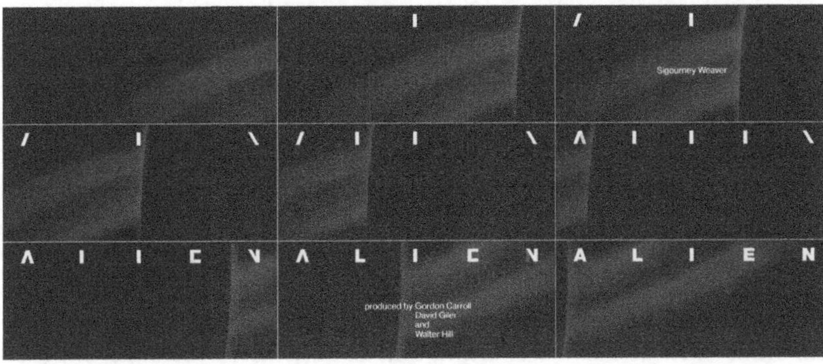

Figure 3.7 Selected title cards from *Alien* (1979), designed by Richard Greenberg

recognizable texts—credits that include the principal cast, production crew, producers, and director—appear on-screen in a continuous series; a full listing of the production will come at the end, after the conclusion of the narrative. All this text (legible and illegible) is superimposed over a composited pan across a dark field with subtle yellow haze. The audience understands this background shot as a long take presenting a dark planet seen from orbit; it behaves as a live action counterpoint to the graphics of the asemic title and semic credits. The separation of photography/text employs the familiar conventions of the figure–ground mode, where text and image occupy entirely distinct 'fields' of interpretation.[11] The differential of semiotic and asemiotic elements emerges gradually, a rhythmic appearance of individual strokes placed one at a time across the top of the screen, while centered below these markings the other credits of the sequence fade on and off as fully legible, coherent texts, an organization of the materials on-screen that renders the *chronic progression* in the main title "ALIEN" as an emergent lexical phenomenon, while the immediacy of the other credits serves as a visual and rhythmic counterpoint.

These same emergent dynamics inform a wide range of title sequence designs, including Michelle Dougherty's design for *Stranger Things* (2016). The coherence of these title cards only emerges from the letters taking their appropriate places to form the TV show's main title: the framing fragments the letterforms, rendering them partially illegible. The fragmentation created by the windowed shards of imagery that provide a background to Joost Korngold's title sequence for *Odyssey in Rome* (2005) creates a similar affect to Dougherty's design, but without the potentially asemic disruption of legibility—the illegible text repeats itself, while other text that is already fully legible appears on-screen. Ben Radatz's design (at MK12) for the James Bond film *Quantum of Solace*

(2008) employs rapidly forming letters whose appearance accelerates the same *chronic progression* as *Alien*, but compressed into a few seconds for each credit. This temporal difference between a slow, gradual emergence and a rapid placement on-screen only to exit a few seconds later distinguishes the *chronic progression* from the mere entrances and exits of Radatz's design.

The familiar figure–ground relationship of text to image interprets the title card texts superimposed over the photographic background as independent from each other: the imagery has no direct relationship to the text. This mode is the most common relationship of text::image in title sequences throughout their history. It has been in use since the 1920s for films such as *Rumba* (Paramount, 1935), where the superimposed text is completely independent of the filmed shadows dancing behind it [Figure 3.8]. The audience reads the text (figure) and sees the image (ground) as entirely independent, unrelated elements. The lack of direct correlation means that the development and meaning of the imagery (background) progresses without concern for what the text might state, allowing the recognition of the 'asemic elements' as actually being illegible text in *Alien*, enabling the 'reading-image' to make conscious this progression towards legibility without confusing what is happening on-screen. The placement at the top of the composition and its continuous presence throughout this opening serves to define the rhythmic addition of elements (appearing symmetrically from both sides of the screen, each element fading on in turn) as a dramatic *entrance* for the main title card. The audience watching the film already knows its title: this awareness reinforces their expectation for what the letters *will* state, making the legibility of this text precede its completion on-screen.

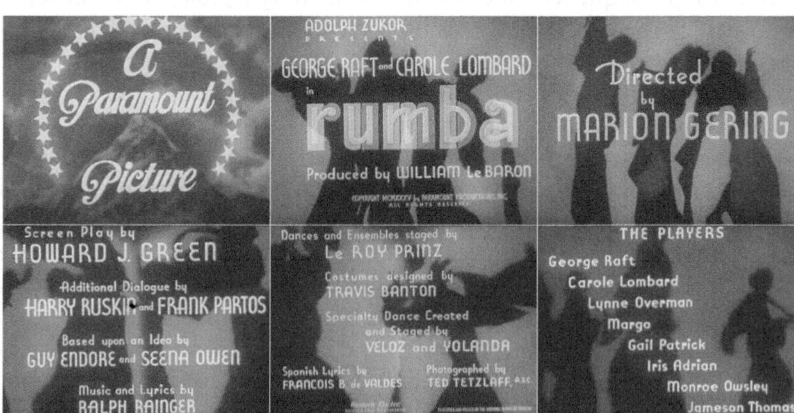

Figure 3.8 All the title cards in *Rumba* (1935)

Lexical engagement dominates perceptual encounter: a higher level of interpretation that alters lower-level encounters based on their correspondence to an expected formal organization of visuality::legibility, the 'reading-image.' This distinction is immediately apparent in the ambivalent status of the disintegrating typography appearing in Danny Yount's title design for *Six Feet Under* (2001), a television drama about a family-run funeral home [Figure 3.9]. The falling-apartness of his text, while suggestive of dysfunction and death, is also a continuous visual feature of the text in these titles—it can be read allegorically, or as a stylistic choice comparable to a preference for serif versus sans serif typefaces—making its expressive articulation questionable. This same disintegration effect appears in another title sequence, *Kingdom Hospital* (2006), designed by Matt Mulder (at Digital Kitchen, the motion design studio responsible for *Six Feet Under*). These integrations of typography with the photographed world-on-film converge on the Deleuzian 'movement-image,' making the necessity for the 'reading-image' apparent: a motion that takes places within the visible world, but which

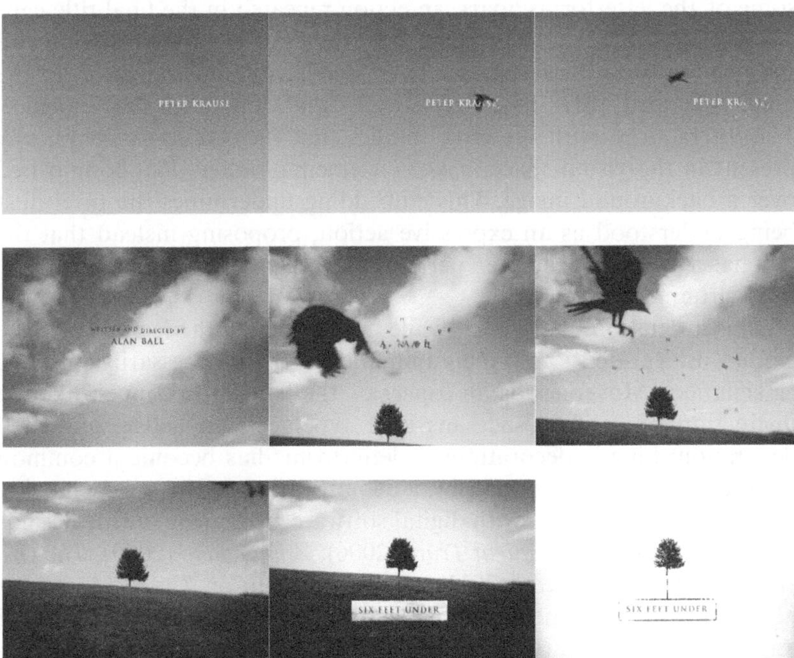

Figure 3.9 Stills from the title sequence for *Six Feet Under* (2001), designed by Danny Yount, showing the first [Top] and last [Middle] credits, and the title card for the main title [Bottom]

retains its connections to lexical and legible textuality. The ambivalence and overlap between *kinetic action* and *chronic progression* in Yount's *Six Feet Under* distinguishes his use from that of Bass's design in *Psycho*. The breaking-up of the letters and the pixelated 'dust' flying away from them is not automatically recognizable as a *particular* expression, distinct from that of the letterforms in themselves. Yount discussed this animation in an interview with Ian Albinson for *Art of the Title* in 2012:

> For the type animation I wanted it to feel like the words turned into ashes and floated away. All we had was *AfterEffects*, but a clever designer named Scott Hudziak figured out a way to use the new particle system in *AE* to do it. Remember: this was 2002, so effects like that were new. He also did an amazing trick to make the type turn to smoke.[12]

Yount's characterization of the typography—a performative activity, happening over time—is what appears on-screen. The text *is* falling apart throughout the design, beginning with the first title card for "PETER KROUSE," where a crow's wing hits the name, breaking some of the letterforms apart, an action repeated in the final title card "WRITTEN AND DIRECTED BY ALAN BALL" that disrupts all the text, causing the letters to fly off-screen for the transition to the main title card "SIX FEET UNDER" that concludes the sequence. The interactions with the crow implies that these texts are physically present in the visual space, *diegetic* elements, rather than composited over a background image. This embedding undermines the pixel dust being understood as an expressive action, proposing instead that the text has a material character, perhaps like pollen, that will blow around its environment.

This animation of the text, while not impacting the legibility of the credits, draws attention to their animation without necessarily cohering as signifiers. Movement is an *aspect* of the letterforms, much like the distinction of serif versus sans serif typefaces, an active, animated decoration; kinetic decorations in letterforms has become a common approach to motion typography, a demonstration of how easy moving typography has become with digital software, appearing in title designs as diverse as *An Inconvenient Truth* (2006), *Zombieland* (2009), *The Girl With the Dragon Tattoo* (2011), *Easy A* (2010), or *The Widowmaker* (2015). Clarity of articulation depends on contrast between being [a] an autonomous feature and [b] an action that implies intentionality—thus, meaning. This process is anticipatory, directing the understanding of these material arrangements of emergent letterforms based on their correspondence to past experience. The 'reading-image' is a kind of rendezvous where the audience understands what they see in terms dictated by what they expect to see *next*, bringing their past experiences with lexical forms to their current encounter, rendering the ambivalent forms in *Humorous Phases of Funny Faces* (1906) as text even before the letterforms exist. These recognitions of type challenge the ambivalent identifications of *asemic* typography for motion pictures: the lexical recognition of these formative elements as *being-typography* mediates engagements with how text and image combine on-screen. The capacity to distinguish between those graphic marks that are language and other marks that are not is a category decision that directs attention to a specific domain of knowledge, one in which the comprehension of letters, words, and meaning derives from enculturation and established expertise,[13] not from the nature of the things encountered.

The formal identification *as* typography—whether static or motion—demonstrates the assertion of the distinction between reading and seeing that shifts between perception and (attempts at) lexical comprehension: separate interpretive processes that specifically becomes apparent in title sequences in the shift from ambivalent marking to lexical form, as in *Humorous Phases of Funny Faces*. The recognition that what initially might have appeared to be an image is instead text—written language—involves the assertion of the dominance of the gaze as an ordering of the world identified by Michel Foucault in *The Birth of the Clinic*.[14] This hierarchy corresponds to shifting category-identifications that allow the audience to impose lexical order: the dominance of language over low-level interpretation links the phenomenal encounter to epistemic knowledge and lexical expertise, a specific tendency towards a materialist understanding of the visible world embodied in the use of sight and vision as metaphor for understanding that establishes the boundaries of comprehension and limits interpretive and conceptual engagement. This ordering function reveals Foucault's understanding of optics as a metaphor that subordinates image to text, where encultured knowledge distinguishes between the recognition of language and its simultaneous apparent structure as graphic marks in *Humorous Phases of Funny Faces*, or the familiar understanding of letter/sound combinations in *Primiti Too Taa*, without a corresponding lexical meaning. The historically technical difficulty with animating typography—simply executing the movements and animorphs of text-on-screen—reveals the identification of lexical form, especially when the linguistic meaning of those forms is unknown or otherwise ambivalent (the 'asemic'), as an assumptive organization that imposes meaning without lexical definitions. Brownie makes this distinction between legibility and signification essential to asemic typography in motion pictures:

> Though asemic signs may themselves defy definition, the state of asemisis is itself meaningful. The apparent presence of a language,

> which challenges viewers to act as readers, combined with the absence of any readable text, has cultural connotations. By being neither figurative nor abstract, asemic writing is difficult to categorize, and asserts its otherness. [...] The otherness of asemic signs may create a level of discomfort for the reader. In challenging the reader to read something that he or she cannot, asemisis reduces the reader to a state of feeling uninformed and uneducated.[15]

The emotional state of the hypothetical reader Brownie describes as "feeling uninformed and uneducated" is a presumptive position that relies on the twin assumptions [a] that the written language is necessarily familiar and [b] that legibility is necessarily the most important criteria for the consideration and engagement with text-on-screen. Foucault's concern with the power of naming and the superficial dominance this action produces corresponds to the identification of lexical form and its invocation of semiotic ordering; however, when the emphasis in this engagement with apparently lexical forms creates expectations for their familiar and understood form, it denies their being 'asemic.' Where [a] has an implicitly colonial dimension, that all languages are identical and the reader should expect to know them automatically; [b] is explicitly Modernist, revealing the demand for ease of reading instrumental to Jan Tschichold's theorization of Modernist graphic design in 1926.[16] Asemic typography draws attention to these issues of *how* lexical form developed in Modernism, masking the encultured and ambivalent aspects of perception and semiosis. This concern with the capacities of language to communicate 'transparently' without the design and typography impeding comprehension is a logical application of the "purity" common to formalist[17] engagements: language *must* communicate; anything that impedes that process *must* be minimized. The reductive process comes to serve the communicative functions of language, but at the same time does so by making the encultured and learned aspects of lexical engagement disappear (apart from the acquisition of semic knowledge of terms and their uses). However, the Modernist conception of legibility is essentially a static one, appropriate only to the immobility of the printed page, fixed at the moment of its production. The letterforms always correspond to a particular arrangement and no other; thus static typography cannot present the 'reading-image.' The recognition of lexical form coupled with its transformative *emergence in time*—the 'reading-image' understood as a specific *chronic progression*—renders the apparently absolute distinction between semiotic and asemiotic typography in static design as an arbitrary distinction without a necessarily fixed point of transition for motion graphics, as *Alien*, *Primiti Too Taa*, and *Humorous Phases of Funny Faces* all demonstrate; neither the stability of letterform outlines nor their legibility are givens for motion typography. The modal shift precisely identifies the temporal development and the transformations that happen over that time to a letterform's morphology and structure.

The problematics of asemic typography particular to the static designs of visual poetry do not apply to the 'reading-image': any momentary illegibility and unintelligibility is countered by the *potential* progression towards an emergent, familiar semiosis, making the proposition of asemic typography a particular affect—itself metastable, comparable to foreign languages and 'nonsense' compositions (such as *Primiti Too Taa*)—rather than an inherent obstacle for motion typography as such. This distinction is more than just an incidental difference; it makes the acknowledgement of *chronic progression* in motion typography a necessary and sufficient condition for separating *motion typography* and the 'reading-image' from the more familiar forms and arrangements of *static typography* employed in both print and graphic design.

Thus, Motion typography that is illegible at one point in its duration may become legible at another, relativizing its asemic dimensions as transitory (not definitive), unlike static typography: indistinguishable or illegible moments of *chronic progression*—the asemic in-betweens of animorphs, for example—do not *remain* asemic. The temporal ordering and transformation that defines the 'reading-image' enables its transition between legibility and illegibility, where the audience's identification of visual forms as *being-text* never leaves those letterforms in asemic limbo. Identifications of typography invoke a different frame of reference than the rest of the pictorial space, always addressing the appearance of text as *potentially* signifying, subject to the demands and concerns of lexical structure and linguistic interpretation. Even momentary transitions that defy the audience's ability to read the text do not result in a recategorization of the text as non-signifying. This identification remains constant: recognizing and identifying the *presence* of language imposes specific conceptual and interpretive demands distinct from those applied to the other visuals appearing on-screen. Transformative shifts into and out of legibility are within the scope of lexical interpretations, a distinction between motion and static typography that explicitly depends on the durative encounter (the literal time of the composition's movements as understood by the audience). This transitive function emerges in the shifts between being graphic marks and being illegible, fragmentary (incomplete) letterforms in *Stranger Things*, *Alien*, and *Humorous Phases of Funny Faces*. The title card presents a text that emerges into comprehension, and in being recognized enables the audience to 'complete' the writing shown. The graphic marks are only genuinely *asemic* prior to their identification as component letterforms, i.e. prior to the identification of the 'reading-image.' The difference between these graphic patterns and the other, decorative graphics that appear in this title sequence is not only an issue of lexical meaning. Because the appearance of the spiral and the flower are continuous while the text emerges as discrete strokes that appear individually, the difference between the textual and the graphic becomes obvious in *chronic progression*, a mode that marks the typo/graphic as different from other marks (decorations, non-lexical flourishes) also appearing on-screen in the early title sequence.

Asemic typography reveals the paradox at the foundation of writing: that it is both a visual form and simultaneously organized and understood through encultured modes that render its visuality invisible—not insignificant, but of only secondary relevance—asemic text brings this hidden visual order back into a position of priority, challenging the lexical order for dominance. Thus is the power of *chronic progression* revealed: the 'reading-image' resolves this basic paradox in the relationship of visual and lexical orders, transforming their defamiliarized and potentially alienating dynamics into the familiar emergence of meaning and recognition, but externalized as the on-screen development into lexical comprehension posed by the gradual revelation of textual forms whose identity as *text* precedes their legibility in semiosis. Violating the hierarchy between *reading–seeing* in this way spreads its differential levels of engagement as the articulation of the motion typography itself. This activity defines the 'reading-image' as it renders the interpretive process as the literal activity of semiotic form shown on-screen. The observations Roland Barthes makes about the metaphoric 'movement' through a series of interpretive levels becomes for motion typography the shifting understanding of a/semic recognition:

> Everything proceeds from spacing out or staggering of articulations. Meaning is born from a combination of non-signifying elements (phonemes, lines); but it is not sufficient to combine these elements to a first degree in order to exhaust the creation of meaning: what has been combined forms aggregates which can combine again among themselves a second, a third time. [...] To defer perception is to engender a new meaning.[18]

In dividing the lexical encounter into its constituent and sequential parts, motion typography exploits an essential feature of reading: that it occurs over time, as a result of a progression through (at its most basic) the immanent collection of discrete marks that are the letterforms; yet in static typography this internal duration is also immobile, unchanging, eternal. The 'reading-image' reveals the difference between these two varieties of textuality: emergent, chronological duration allows the expansion of the immanent recognition *textuality* to become an active part of the formal presentation and meaning of the work. In separating the essential lexical procedures of identification and recognition from the immanent category assignment 'text,' the durative aspects of reading become a part of its material structure, apparent in the morphology of motion typography itself. In discussing this dynamic process, Barthes identified the *time* of encounter as an essential problematic for the stability of identifications—their legibility—that does not present difficulties for its audience, who understand the dynamic as an externalization of discourse as/in design:

> The lexia is only the wrapping up of a sematic volume, the crest line of a plural text, arranged like a berm of possible (but controlled, attested to by a systematic reading) meanings under the flux of discourse: the lexia and its units will thereby form a kind of polyhedron faceted by the word, the group of words, the sentence or paragraph, i.e. with the language which is its "natural" excipient.[19]

The 'reading-image' expands the modal articulations of static text identified as language, moving backwards from high-level organization into the abyssal of perception and an immanence of form and design. This displacement between immanent recognition and the emergence of legibility articulates the significance of the typo/graphics in the experiential encounter, a modulation of lexical recognitions throughout the extension of the title sequence, serving to identify that collection of texts as a singular, contained unit apart from the rest of the motion picture. Visuality for motion typography articulates the 'reading-image' in a reiteration of the hierarchy appearing in static texts as the relations of word to sentence to paragraph to page, becoming in motion the features of scale, placement, emergence, and durative articulation on-screen. As in ancient art where the most important figures are larger and more visually prominent than their less important counterparts, the placement and size of text-on-screen articulates this same hieratic importance, expressed not only through the scale of letterforms but in their emergence to legibility: the title for *Alien* in Greenberg's design actually appears in all caps at the top of the screen, *above* the rest of the text, while the lettering for the actors' credits is a combination of uppercase and lowercase typography, visually half the size of the main title in scale and unquestionably *below* it. In contrast, the main title is a continuous presence in *Stranger Things*, surrounding and containing the other credits of the sequence; the falling-into-place that renders the title coherent is not an emergence, but an imposition of order that makes the design become comprehensible (the letterforms have been recognizable throughout the sequence).

In serving to identify the title sequence as a pseudo-independent unit, these modes reinforce its peritextual[20] segmentation of/as 'opening' apart from the rest of the narrative; it is a mode of articulation that reinforces and rearticulates the title sequence as such, a graphic analogue to the role of music in separating the title sequence from other sequences that follow.[21] This compartmentalization of enunciation is particularly evident in Richard Greenberg's title designs, a stylistic reflection of his handling of the asemic aspects of typography within the title sequence; however, as an articulative practice asemic type is not limited to his work. The apparently asemic dimension of the text at the start, and the progressive appearance and shift towards legible completion defers reading through transformations of immanent form. Asemic elements in motion typography displace the 'wrapping-up' of semiotic engagement, delaying its progression to express other elements of meaning through the letterforms themselves, which are presented as specific independent moments of enunciation on-screen—not a potential dimension, but immanent—in visual activities that render visuality as an excess which modifies and accents the familiar dimensions of lexical presentation. The 'reading-image' entails dynamic transformation, a metonymic implication made through the animation rather than in the text itself: in the dynamic motion of the logo for WTOP-TV that homologously suggests that the TV station has dynamic programming. While in Greenberg's design for *Alien* the emergent, shape-changing text literally hangs over the characters in the same way that the alien creature will stalk them in the narrative to follow, while the crowding and enveloping credits in Dougherty's *Stranger Things* suggests the unknown and mysterious threats that stalk the children who are the protagonists. Peritextual organizations that integrate the opening shot of the film into the credit sequence in the Prologue Mode[22] do not preclude anticipation of later events in that narrative through the presentation of the text shown on-screen. This secondary level of annunciation arises from the recognition of a rhetorical dimension beyond that of lexical form, requiring an interpretation that engages with the duration of the animation, rather than apprehending it as a purely atemporal, semiotic presentation of meaning. While this additional dimension of significance is a potential aspect of static typography, it is explicitly deployed as a part of the enunciations of motion typography in the 'reading-image,' an additional and essential dimension articulated through the motion and *chronic progression* of animation, distinguishing the interpretation of motion graphics at an essential and foundational level of engagement from that of graphic design.

Notes

1 Brownie, B. *Transforming Type: New Directions in Motion Typography* (New York: Bloomsbury, 2015) pp. 7–11.

2 Heidegger, M. *Being and Time* trans. Joan Stambaugh (Albany: The State University of New York Press, 1996) section 172, p. 161.

3 Brownie, B. *Transforming Type: New Directions in Motion Typography* (New York: Bloomsbury, 2015) p. 55.

4 Federici, F. "Is asemic writing a zero-point writing? (Asemic Draft in progress n.3)" *Utsanga.it* no. 15. (March 2018) ed. Francesco Aprile and Cristiano Caggiula utsanga.it/federici-is-asemic-writing-zero-point-writing/ March 27, 2018, retrieved April 10, 2018.

5 Heidegger, M. *Being and Time* trans. Joan Stambaugh (Albany: The State University of New York Press, 1996) section 206, p. 191.

6 Lupton, E. and Miller, A. *Design Writing Research: Writing on Graphic Design* (New York: Phaidon, 1996) p. 14.

7 Schwitters, K. "Ursonate (1922–1932)" *Kurt Schwitters: PPPPPP: Poems Performance Pieces Proses Plays Poetics* ed. and trans. Jerome Rothenberg and Pierre Joris (Philadelphia: Temple University Press, 1993) pp. 52–80.

8 Barthes, R. *The Responsibility of Forms* (Berkeley: The University of California Press, 1985), p. 137–141.

9 Holland, J. *Hidden Order: How Adaptation Builds Complexity* (Reading: Perseus Books, 1995) pp. 53–56.

10 Foucault, M. *The Archaeology of Knowledge* (New York: Pantheon, 1972) p. 88.

11 Betancourt, M. *Semiotics and Title Sequences: Text–Image Composites in Motion Graphics* (New York: Routledge Focus, 2017).

12 Tagudin, A. and Albinson, I. "*Six Feet Under* (2001)" *Art of the Title* posted November 12, 2012, retrieved April 28, 2018 artofthetitle.com/title/six-feet-under/

13 Foucault, M. *The Birth of the Clinic* (New York: Vintage, 1975).

14 Foucault, M. *The Birth of the Clinic* (New York: Vintage, 1975) p. xiii.

15 Brownie, B. *Transforming Type: New Directions in Motion Typography* (New York: Bloomsbury, 2015) p. 55.

16 Tschichold, J. *The New Typography* (Berkeley: University of California Press, 1998).

17 Golden, W. "Type is to read" *The Visual Craft of William Golden* ed. Cipe Pineles Golden, Kurt Weihs and Robert Stunsky (New York: George Braziller, 1962) pp. 13–35.

18 Barthes, R. *The Responsibility of Forms* (Berkeley: The University of California Press, 1985) pp. 141–142.

19 Barthes, R. *S/Z: an essay* (New York: Hill and Wang, 1974) p. 14.

20 Stanitzek, G. "Texts and Paratexts in Media" *Critical Inquiry* no. 32. (Autumn 2005) pp. 27–42.

21 Betancourt, M. *Synchronization and Title Sequences: Audio-Visual Semiosis in Motion Graphics* (New York: Routledge Focus, 2017) pp. 122–123.

22 Betancourt, M. *Title Sequences as Paratexts: Narrative Anticipation and Recapitulation* (New York: Routledge Focus, 2018) pp. 128–138.

4 Conclusions

Motion versus Static Design

Analyzing typography on-screen is a complex and metastable affair of overlapping interpretive modes whose engagements happen simultaneously at different levels of conscious attention: first in simple terms as 'meaning,' and then with greater complexity as the 'reading-image,' in addressing relationships of text–image composites, and finally in the intratextual realm to oversee *narrative function*. Immanent encounters remain within the familiar scope of static design, but *kinesis* modulates time in motion graphics to expand the potential significations of typography in ways that undermine its unitary linguistic identification and superficially secure ontological status, rendering the immanent a transactional moment in an ongoing emergence. In contradistinction to graphic design's use of typography, how motion graphics employ movement on-screen and development over time in the *kinetic*, *graphic*, and *chronic* modes is superficially tied to its historical relationship with established, static design methodologies (*graphic expression*), but this connection does not alter the absolute difference created by *durative* time and the motion-visual composition of the screen acting simultaneously at different levels of engagement.

Formal identities are *mutable qua kinesis*, unstable contingencies that cannot be assumed. Separating motion typography from static design is ultimately about the technical *potential* to animate text. The implications of motion in static designs are specifically that—suggestions which mark the transformation into motion graphics: graphic design does not have the capacity to change appearance and legibility over time—that would require a change in form, i.e. *movement*—real, cinematic motion is not the same as the *metaphoric* allusion of static designs. The dynamic of visuality::legibility that defines the 'reading-image' asserts *kinesis* as the necessary and sufficient criteria for defining motion typography in the capacity to display movement on-screen.

The simplicity of motion typography, its obviousness, makes this ontological consideration harder, but more valuable. One of the greatest difficulties in its analysis is the temporal dimension that makes all acts of *reading* more than just a momentary or passing point of critical engagement, but redolent of a process whose subjects and understandings are neither fixed nor precise for motion pictures in the ways that they inherently are for static compositions. This overlap with other *temporal* arts makes the role of typography in motion pictures an entirely different and in/dependent development that must exceed the scope and parameters of static typography and design.

There are only limited types of motion pictures where concerns from commercial, fictive cinema overlap with those of the avant-garde, and in which design and typography have a central position; these sets of dynamic and immanent features informs the theoretical utility of title sequences. Title sequences facilitate analysis by escaping from conceptually simplistic definitions of formal taxonomies and ontological assumptions about typography to consider the more complex modes that inform its material distinctions. Because cinematic theories have not considered motion graphics, they have ceded that territory to the approaches of graphic design, resulting in these contemporary challenges to historical motion pictures as digital convergence allows the innovative and exceptional methods of formerly marginal productions—such as music videos, title sequences, VFX animations—into a more prominent position, as forerunners to the reversion of live action into a specialized case of animated image, subject to the same plastic deformations and transformations as any other picture.

Digital technology makes these developments increasingly pressing.[1] Motion typography is prominent in contemporary digital design, but remains constrained by the visuality::legibility dynamic in a limited range of potentials developed by analogue animation processes: hand-animation, optical printing, and video processing. The resentiment of non-narrative concerns with animation and the plastic nature of representation threaten the established domains and definitions of the cinematic: they undermine its received theories of discourse and photographic indexicality.[2] However, it is not technology but *kinesis* that distinguishes the peculiar semiotics of *motion graphics* that allows a delay in recognitions of typographic semiosis (and its assertion of order), without undermining or challenging it, by presenting this process of lexical recognition as the emergence *into* legibility. The importance of disassociating motion typography from these predations of technology necessitated an engagement with the 'reading-image' via its historical development, rather than in primarily contemporary designs. Their constancy distinguishes motion typography from static design over the twentieth century, demonstrating these particular modes are precisely independent of the technical innovations that make them common.

Reading/Discourse

Reading is a particular engagement with letterforms guided by the audience's familiarity with the discourse of written and textual languages, a distinct and parallel mode of engagement from their visual perceptions: the immanent encounter resolves the visuality::legibility dynamic into a 'natural' hierarchy where legibility always dominates, and the ease of reading is the only 'real' concern.[3] Interpretive processes create meaning dependent on an always already established larger framework of historical knowledge—encultured past experience and learned expertise—that when employed directs and selects the appropriate protocols to render *reading* a meeting with an apparently inert, fixed discourse bounded by traditional strictures. This issue of recognition begins with denotation in the immanent, *static* image as an articulation of 'content,' the thing shown (words), *prior* to recognizing *anything else*, such as movement. Discourse emerges as definitive in the separation between the recognition of language, and the ability to identify and read the contents presented. In considering these *expressive* dynamics, semiotician Roman Jakobson's *poetic function* proposes the special problem of emotive significance as a crucial inflection that alters meaning on phonic, grammatical, and lexical levels[4] in both speech and static designs. These limits to enunciation also apply in typo/graphy and visual, concrete, and asemic poetry generally, linking them with the temporal and durative presentation of moving type on-screen due to its capacity for a shifting and ambivalent emergence in/out of legibility, familiarity, and stable identity as *being-type*. Consequently, the differences in discourse between static and motion typography can be challenging to articulate since the historical tendency is for cinema study to deny the significance of text except in narrowly defined ways connected to and constrained by *narrative functions* such as character, drama, and plot (*fabula*), while graphic design simultaneously makes metaphoric claims about being a *temporal* organization comparable to the chronological, durative nature of motion pictures.

Critical dimensions of motion typography via the 'reading-image' derive from the capacity to externalize (and thus render immanent) an internal, subjective process of recognition *as* the presentation on-screen. A reader's decision to understand lexical form arises not from the work but in the engagement chosen: *any* viewer can engage *any* work visually instead of lexically. This recognition opposes traditional, even conservative misconceptions of audiences as inherently passive viewers, acted upon and manipulated by a process that dictates their understanding.

Contra this traditional view, the entirety of the work fundamentally depends on the audience's activity and engagement—even at almost unconscious, autonomous 'levels'—making the received understanding of cinema, the movement of imagery, and the medium of 'motion pictures' a highly contingent phenomenon with specific socio-political implications for any media theory or praxis: the conceptual schema of an always already *active* 'model reader' is necessary to the conception of the 'reading-image' as an externalized presentation of a discourse about perceptual recognitions-interpretations constituting lexical forms.

These choices determine even the lowest level of perceptual recognition, historically assumed to be essential for the discourse of motion pictures, the *naturalistic denotation* of photography, whose indexicality realist cinema understands as an ontological link to 'the real.' This connection of the photographed image to what it apparently 'contains' is not a 'given'; it depends instead on the internalized role of past experience, and a willingness to consider the mediation of cinematic realism as equivalent to selectively limited aspects of experiential encounters.[5] Denotation is *not* an ontological identification, but an interpreted conclusion. The 'reading-image' is a philosophical investigation that becomes the proximate encounter—a procedural demonstration made to expand the autonomous and internalized activity of recognition and interpretation into the emergence of letterforms, allowing the transition from illegible to legible to become an expressive *subject*.

Typo/graphic dynamics emerge from this encultured discourse; they are never *only* about legibility as letterforms and words, but this distinction only becomes apparent when the visual dimensions of text challenges the meaning of its contents. Type choices, layout, images, and other graphics function invisibly, guiding and enabling the navigation of the page and screen in ways that typically only become apparent in their failure—those rare, marginal situations when these other dimensions challenge a transparent legibility for dominance. In describing the *kinetic*, *graphic*, and *chronic* modes of the 'reading-image,' what unites them is precisely this shifted discourse: they are alternatives to the narrative and realist foundations of Giles Deleuze's 'movement-image.' His attempt to theorize the articulation of a realist image-world through the narrational articulation of its material presentation differs from historical accounts of realism only by *not* assuming an ontological link to reality, but it does not extend beyond the limits of its considered sources in feature-length fictional films—the "great films," taken as an unquestionable given.[6] In place of a referential basis in the fictive world-on-film, the 'reading-image' describes a series of expressive functions that augment but do not replace the lexicality of text: animation impacts and alters the meaning of the words themselves, but this distension does not obviate their semiosis. It is an externalization of how the audience's *internal* reading proceeds in/as the presentation of text-on-screen, relying on the motion picture's innate and automatic mediation of time to allow a separation between visuality::legibility that are always conjoined in static typography. The *kinetic*, *graphic*, and *chronic* modes allow a delay in typographic semiosis (and its assertion of discursive order) without undermining or challenging that significance by presenting the process of lexical recognition as the emergence *into* legibility. This rupture of apparently fixed, stable semiosis to become instead a representation of the audience's interpretive process (informed by the discourse which makes meaning possible)—not a fictive presentation of a narrative—marks a fundamental incompatibility between the 'reading-image' and Deleuze's proposals parallel to the separation of the *crediting* and *narrative functions* in title sequences.[7]

The Role of *Kinesis*

Movement is both a technical aspect of motion pictures and a specific perceptual understanding of the imagery encountered. This duality of movement on-screen in all animated and live action motion pictures depends on the same, essential technological rendering that becomes 'invisible,' masked by its disappearance into/as the motion of the shot that enables the high-level organization of sequences into narrative, drama, and plot. The erasure of motion typography mirrors this refusal of motion, an endemic lacuna in media study, revelatory of motion graphics' historical origins in those marginal types of cinema that parallel the literary concerns of *cinema=narrative* approaches: the abstract, avant-garde (or 'experimental') film's historical concerns with rendering a subjective engagement immanent on-screen. The 'reading-image' and its non-narrative, non-lexical engagement with language belong to this tradition.

The common heritage of the 'advanced arts' in the first decades of the twentieth century reveals historical continuities which are developed in commercial motion graphics: the avant-gardes were in a search for universal languages capable of conquering the babbling discord that divided nations and peoples[8]; the birth of semiotics in Switzerland answered to this same call, offering a systematic understanding of what were taken to be the uniform, structural foundations of language.[9] Later critiques challenged these presumptions, noting how the entanglement of interpretations and justifications build up in a circular logic, validating their conclusions on the basis of their own propositions, inventing meaning without reference to the object of consideration.[10] The avant-garde search for a 'visual language' led to works that articulated their meaning through visual structures crafted through an organization analogous to musical structures that build significance through rhythmic, harmonic, and graphic orchestrations of form in static compositions. This heritage becomes literal in motion pictures: there is no need for any *metaphoric* suggestion of these concerns when they can actually be presented on-screen synchronized with soundtracks. Instead of looking to conceive of the screen as an imaginary window into a fictive world whose space-environment is an expression of the dynamic between naturalism::stylization familiar from realist dramas, the 'reading-image' draws attention to *kinesis* on-screen as a field in which complex representational and lexical operations can occur, testing and challenging our ability to create meaning and significance in a dynamic relationship between immanence and past experience.

Changing the conception of motion picture from shot to frame, from transparent window to opaque screen,[11] is the heritage of avant-garde cinema. All three modes of 'reading-image' define a semiotic process immanent in/as the 'making sense' of letterforms via *kinesis.* Their distinctive engagements with the non-lexical dimensions of typography and design proceed from their foundations in static typography and the printed page, but exceed them because the addition of motion is transformative, allowing the presentation of interpretive processes through animated motion. Philosopher-filmmaker Daniel Barnett describes these interpretive and analytic methods of engagement and discourse in *Movement as Meaning in Experimental Film* as dimensions of the same basic process:

> If you simply describe meaning as *what goes on in the time it takes to know where to go* with something, then the difference among how we come to understand the meanings of words, pictures, music, or for that matter when we experience the whole previous array, bundled into a movie, can be compared on an even field—an even field that allows us to tease out useful similarities and distinctions about the referential character of each.[12]

The apparently obvious role of *time* in comprehension is a dimension that motion pictures do not share with the static, fixed format of printed text and the fully immanent appearance of graphic design. Instead of the page, the temporal stream of pictures in a movie (that may include words) presents itself as an 'event' happening on-screen both immediately in the sound::image unit and emerging over time,[13] which offers the possibility of dramatic transformations and ejects the typically internal process of 'figuring out' what something *is* into the revelation of that thing on-screen. The 'time of discovery' for static design defines the recognitions and assignments of value combined into words, sentences, lines, paragraphs—and on into the higher-level orders of pages, chapters and books—but in cinema, internal and instant decisions rendering text immanent can (and do) expand into the 'reading-image' as an exploration of the articulation's expressiveness, rather than a fixed progression into an established structural hierarchy (the printed page).

Lexical order dominates perception. Sensory experience determines the initial parameters for meaning in motion pictures, and is the vehicle for those recognitions blended with the quotations and allusions that produce it. Although *motion* changes the relationship between legibility and lexical form, it does not eliminate the immanent identification of *being-language*—whether they are known or unknown, the recognition of shapes as *being-letterforms* (or *being-pictographs*)—renders an expectation of meaning and thus of the intentional ordering that accompanies it; 'naming' (denotation) is an imposed interpretation.[14] *Kinesis* changes this recognition process, destabilizing the interpretation to focus on its chronological emergence into familiarity: the potential for the audience to eventually *read* what the words say.

The hierarchy of *reading–seeing–hearing* creates an aura of textuality that overrides visuality, incorporating the material letterforms into words and then denying the words themselves to confront their known meaning through an indexical relationship relying on established fluency (past experience). All freedom from imposed orders must be actively asserted, a demand that only the audience can make or meet. Semiotician Umberto Eco addresses this 'perception problem' in his book *Kant and the Platypus*, recognizing that even if we treat perception as a semiotic process, it does not remove the more basic issue of the perception itself:

> The fact that a perception may be successful precisely because we are guided by the notion that the phenomenon is hypothetically understood as a sign [...] does not eliminate the problem of how we perceive it.[15]

Identifying *things as what they appear to be* is the end product of this encountering process, producing both reality and realism, a recognition of apparent ontology for images of all types that draws the philosophy of being into the realm of epistemology, knowledge, that semiotics also describes. The refusals of visuality in serious philosophical and art historical analysis of language and text are compounded by the issues of perception that *visuality* and *kinesis* necessarily raise. The imposition of lexical order is at the same time a recourse to encultured knowledge. Motion typography expounds on this established, familiar capacity of *text* to externalize abstract information and knowledge to animate/impose a separation between *recognizing* language and *reading* its encoded statements, but texts are typically considered for their legibility, rather than the expressions created through their animation and activity on-screen independent of these lexical functions (identity as words with their meanings). Therein lies the difficulty.

Kinesis introduces delays into category assignment and changes the lexical dynamics to have an active, immediate character: the 'events' of motion pictures always happen for their audiences in the *present* (at the moment of perception). Parsing these sensation/perceptions via *kinesis* into significances and insignificances attracts, deflects, and organizes *attention*, but unlike everyday experience, in motion pictures the time encapsulated on-screen can be rewound, replayed, reconsidered, allowing audiences to engage their internal, subjective activities productive of a particular result. This ability of motion pictures to encapsulate and modulate *time* and model the process of lexical engagement as a literal progression on-screen allows motion typography to represent via *kinesis* those recognitions that become *reading*, distended and arrayed for consideration as an experience which renders meaning: thus marking its separation from the organization of fixed elements *qua* typography (the *being-language* that semiosis engages). In allowing the organization of a text as the gradual, emerging series of actions performed in making sense of that text, animated typography matches the other aspects of motion pictures in which what is shown on-screen corresponds to an experience in the world, mediated *and* idealized. This articulation of what historically has been an internal, subjective activity defines the 'reading-image' and differentiates it from mere reading of static text, suggesting that a "gignomenological law of identity"[16] inheres in all semiosis: a general interpretation is not merely a summary of a certain group of past experiences, but offers/contains potentials that are matched by similar experiences and interpretations *in the future*. The 'reading-image' prioritizes a particular kind of lexicality for its audience, a metaphysical 'realism of the mind' indexically linked to 'the real,' yet disconnected from fictional worlds or the superficial appearances of everyday things.

Constraints on Semiosis

Realism distinguishes the uses of motion typography in commercial films and videos from those of avant-garde media works: the invisible adherence to the protocols and formal structures of realist cinema are apparent in the demand for an integration of typography and photography so that the lexical dimensions of text do not produce a disruptive counterpoint that challenges the narrative diegesis. Digital technology has turned what were 'expensive' (labor-intensive) animation techniques—thus, rare and unusual, often only appearing in avant-garde media—into commonplace practices as a result of commercial demands for lower cost, increased control, and greater efficiency in production and post-production, making the 'reading-image' more common and potentially creating an illusion that it depends on digital tools. The specifically historical framework of this analysis demonstrated that the 'reading-image' is a feature of movement understood semiotically.

Digital tools have changed the conditions and intransient potentials of analogue video and historical optical printing into easily generated and controlled animation techniques, with the result that what were formerly highly complex animations of motion typography are no longer exceptional but mundane. As the break-up of frames in film creates the potential for motion, the encoding of imagery as digital data offers the potential to radically change the duration, composition, and progression of the resulting imagery on-screen simply by altering the parameters of the digitally encoded information in ways that are literally impossible with analogue media, creating what Steven Shaviro terms "post-cinema."[17] Digital media is not a discrete technology where one type of material, *motion pictures*, remains entirely different and separate from other types of material, *books*, *sound recordings*. The digital encoding of all these as binary information processed and electronically rendered into superficially different, human-readable forms—data only differentiated by its decoding—facilitates transformations and shifts that were literally impossible with analogue media; the historical relationship between the emergence of Shaviro's "post-cinema" and the developments of digital animation and motion graphics lies with the contemporary collapse of *all* motion pictures (including cinema and television) into computer imaging.[18] Attempts to render the immaterial digital as a physicality are a commonplace feature of contemporary society, a convergence of virtual processes and the real world that is increasingly obvious in everyday experience.[19] Computational processing is not limited to cinema or motion pictures; it is part of the everyday, the environment, and embedded in the texture of life itself.[20] The markers of cinema's specificity—photography's ontological connection to reality, forcefully theorized by André Bazin—and its dispositive are not limited to only the construction of a subjective position, but include the heterogeneous constellation of discourses, institutions, legal propositions, and philosophical arguments that provide a paradigm whose crumbling appears to be a state of collapse as new heuristic frameworks and tools emerge (creating "post-cinema").[21] And yet these tools are employed for increasingly photorealistic productions, creating ever more convincing resemblances to 'the real' that lies at the foundations of Bazin's proposal: the appearance of what a viewer might see were they personally a witness to the events shown on-screen.

The proximate and exacting control over individual pixels in digital images amplifies potentials for the on-screen manipulation already familiar from the history of motion graphics. Unlike the photographs

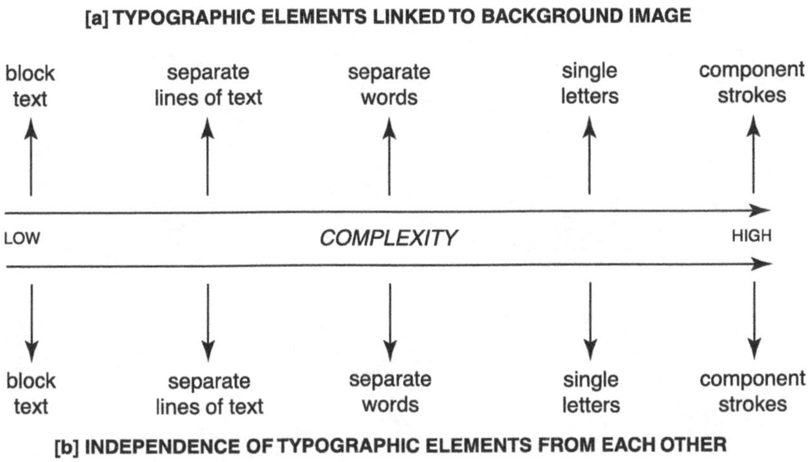

Figure C.1 Diagram of the two parallel variables in Barbara Brownie's study of motion typography, *Transforming Type*

of film, the digital imagery shown on-screen is composed from discrete samples that can be individually addressed, engaged, and altered in ways identified by Barbara Brownie's taxonomy in *Transforming Type: New Directions in Motion Typography*. Her analysis employs two high-level variables that [a] describe motions of either individual letterforms or entire words, paralleled by [b] the degree of independence each element or letterform has from the others [Figure C.1]. Her typology describes the convergent role of animation, optical printing, avant-garde film, and graphic design in commercial title design, not distinguished technologically, but by the extent to which the typography has been 'embedded' in the apparent space of the background imagery, allowing the text to become a part of the realist 'space' shown on-screen; thus, her system assumes the realist construction of its images, making it poorly suited to recognizing the externalization of thought processes in the morphology and structure of motion typography as they develop on-screen. Digital production enables the (re)emergence of animation as the central technical/theoretical concern for motion pictures (cinema) in general,[22] making the historical relationships between early film and contemporary digital technology theoretically important: it acknowledges the continuity rather than the rupture posed by computer technology, the banality of digital convergence.

Twentieth-century theorizations of cinema kept animation and live action critically separate, but interpreted through a shared cultural construct: *realism*. The *cinema=narrative* relationship still operates

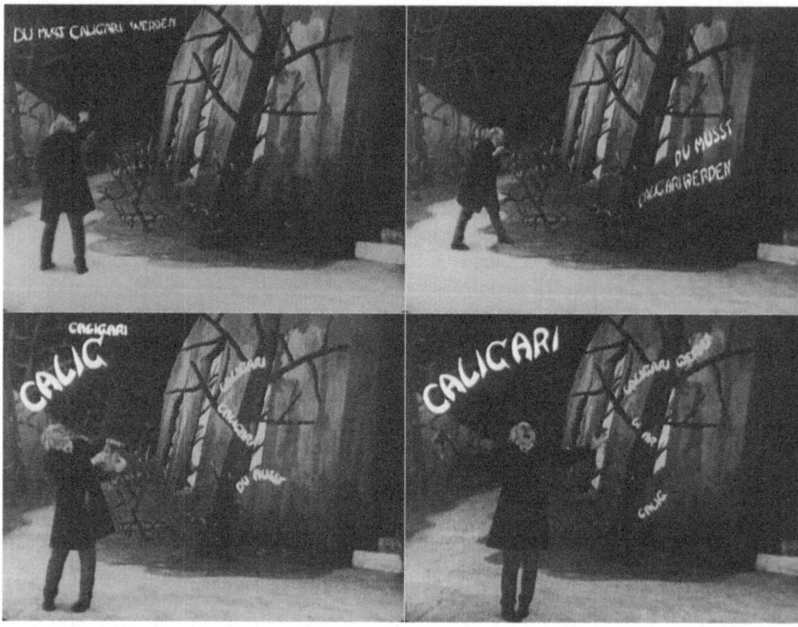

Figure C.2 Stills stating "DU MUSST CALIGARI WERDEN" ("YOU MUST BECOME CALIGARI") from *The Cabinet of Dr. Caligari* (1919), showing extra-diegetic typography

in digital cinema, a tacit aesthetic-ideological constraint that keeps attention directed to the story being presented on-screen. In attending to the demands of *fabula* and diegesis, the *narrative function* of typography works against its engagement as an expression of consciousness—except in the relatively rare forms of *extra-diegetic typography* where the text-on-screen is precisely associated with the mental state of the characters that share that visual space,[23] as pioneered in *The Cabinet of Dr. Caligari* (1919) [Figure C.2]. *What* appears can be analyzed, critiqued, challenged, but the question of mimesis itself is contingent on an established, *a priori* range of naturalism::stylization. Realism is a powerful ideology in cinema, almost inescapable: in instances of typographic–narrative convergence, the *narrative function* dominates the expressiveness of the text. To understand it as an expression of character subjectivity, the word must become a part of the diegetic world-on-screen. Each superimposed text that states "DU MUSST CALIGARI WERDEN" ("YOU MUST BECOME CALIGARI") appears either floating in the air or following the contours of a tree as the director returns to his home—although these words are superimposed, a 'camera trick,' the actor's performance demands they be understood as immanent, a diegetic fact, imaginary yet actually present in the on-screen dramatic space (thus *extra*-diegetic).

The 'reading-image' is countered by the conventional subjectivity of this shot, its realism, in what Deleuze identified as a 'perception-image.' What the viewers see corresponds to narration *about* perception within the drama; the antipathy between the 'reading-image' and Deleuze's 'movement-image' is absolute. Understanding these changing relations as a familiar and easily made distinction separates the 'reading-image' from narration, as Eco explained in his discussion of drama in *Interpreting Serials*:

> With words, a phonic object stands for other objects made with different stuff. In the mise-en-scene, an object, first recognized as a real object, is then assumed as a sign in order to refer to another object (or to a class of objects) whose constitutive stuff is the same as that of the representing object.[24]

Unlike the 'reading-image,' where the lexical order invoked by the opposition between the material-of-the-fictional-world and the materiality-of-language is ambivalently conjoined, the extra-diegetic presentation of character perception on-screen renders those visible elements and texts *not* language, but symbolic form: the immanent demonstration of character subjectivity; in *The Cabinet of Doctor Caligari* psychosis manifests in/as the word. The meaning for "DU MUSST CALIGARI WERDEN" *is* madness, rather than the standard semiotic interpretations of the text itself; understanding what these words symbolize requires a denial of them as language and their treatment instead as part of the mise-en-scène within the fictive space of the drama. This assimilation of text to objecthood (thus coinciding with realist dramatization of this character's mental state) renders the *significance* and *expressive* nature of that text secondary to its *narrative function*. The style and shape of the lettering in *The Cabinet of Dr. Caligari*, much like the stylized environment, is Expressionist. Its form is not indicative of unique particular statements, demonstrating instead a consistency with the rest of the narrative order: it is a reflection of a realist morphology where the emphasis falls on the stylized rather than the naturalistic presentation of events and actions.

The 'reading-image' becomes an instance of what Michel Foucault argued about knowledge and understanding: that vision is equated with mental activity, embodied in the "empirical gaze." His ideological construction of sight/vision as descriptive of knowledge and understanding finds immanent form in the 'reading-image' as a visualization of thought processes.[25] The cultural meaning of *sight* and *insight* reveals a foundational mediation between the encounter in perception and its interpretation as a *statement*. This dynamic shifts enunciations available for consideration to those already contained by an established interpretive order: in *The Cabinet of Doctor Caligari* this order is provided by the *narrative function* that makes the dramatic significance of the typography immediately apparent to the audience. The dual roles of knowledge—*intra*textuality and *inter*textuality—in this example creates the stability and 'naturalness' that hides the lexical shifts producing these interpretations. Realism is central to this process. The 'natural' world-on-screen relies on identifications of immanent, empirical objects and motions that resemble those in the physical world.

The encounter with lexical structures thus depends on the audience's recognition of their relationship to the rest of the materials shown on-screen. It is an immanent decision separating internalities from externalities—a division between those elements that are assumed to belong *within* the world-on-screen and those that are external to it—that creates the dynamic of naturalism::stylization and the realism it defines. The difference between 'reading-image' and Deleuze's proposals reflects this distinction of diegetic and non-diegetic. The problematics of these terms and their applications in cinema are typically hidden or ignored except in specific circumstances, themselves situations where stylization dominates naturalism,[26] such as *The Cabinet of Doctor Caligari*. The placement of language within diegetic space, as with the physical embedding of the title card typography in the live action shots at the start of *The Adventures of Baron Munchausen* (1988) [Figure C.3], reveals how the later digital integration of text and image in films such as *Sherlock Holmes* (2009) or *Sucker Punch* (2011) [Figure C.4] is simply a logical extension of realist demands already operative in commercial productions that require an assimilation of *all* stylization (of which superimposed and composited texts are an explicit example) into the diegetic, naturalistic construct of *fabula*.

Hybrids such as motion graphics that bridge the differences between design, animation, avant-garde film, and commercial narratives were historically neglected and ignored as insignificant; the realist demand appears through the opposition between the *crediting* and *narrative* functions of typography. The integration of typography within that visual space—the world-on-screen—assumes a skeuomorphic character at its most extreme: the literal integration of typography with image in such a way that the text and the picture are interchangeable. The digital transformation of diegetic elements in *Sucker Punch* is anticipated by the purely hand-drawn type-images of Terry Gilliam's design for *The Life of Brian* (1979), where the credits coexist as cartoons accompanying collages taken from both the classical art history of Greece and Rome, and imagery taken from Gustave Dore's *Divine Comedy* illustrated books

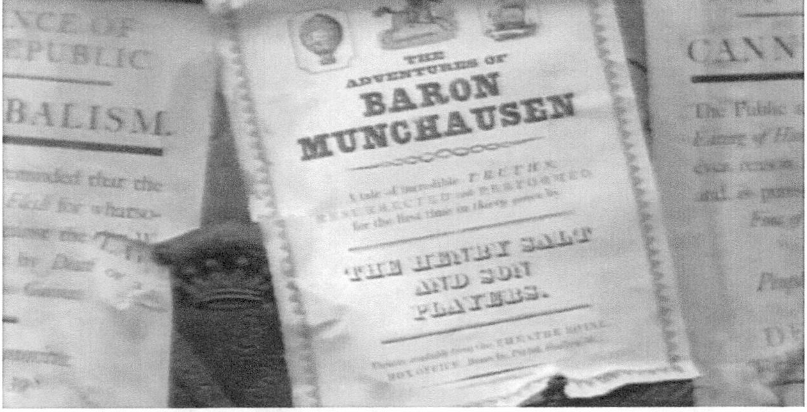

Figure C.3 Still frame showing the film title as a live action element in *The Adventures of Baron Munchausen* (1988)

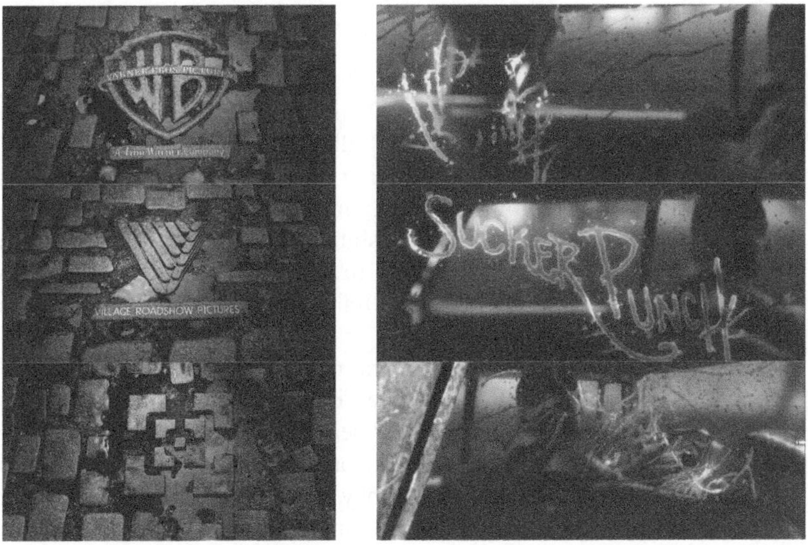

Figure C.4 [Left] Studio logos embedded in live action footage from the opening to *Sherlock Holmes* (2009); [Right] typography animated and integrated into the live action in *Sucker Punch* (2011)

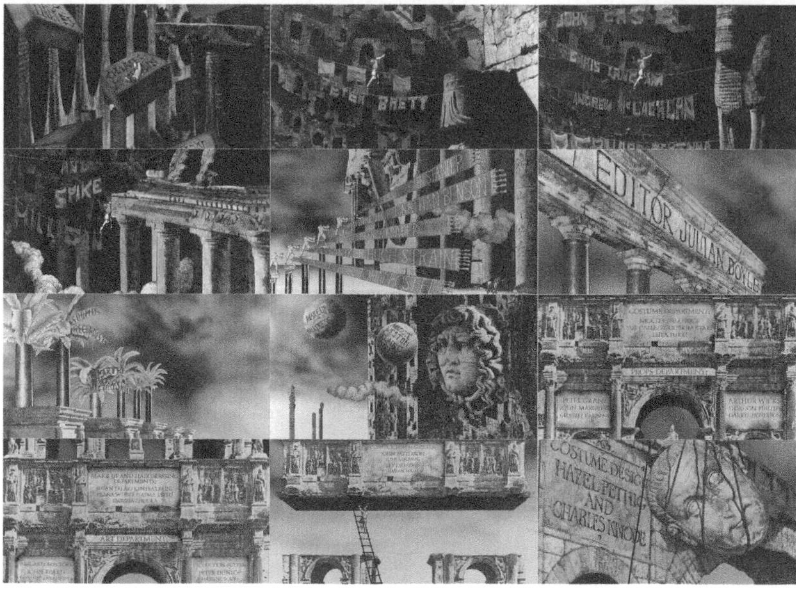

Figure C.5 Selected title cards from *The Life of Brian* (1979)

published in the nineteenth century. This embedding of credits within the animated panorama [Figure C.5] allows their refusal—the denial that the words are lexical—by embracing their ambivalent alternative as mere graphics. The resulting instability makes the challenge of reading at the same time a clear decision to shift categorical assignment from image to language. In choosing how to see the titles, the distinctions between visuality::legibility become a reflection of the audience's desire to see pictures or read words.

The realist demand apparent in the narrative significance of "DU MUSST CALIGARI WERDEN" [see Figure C.2, page 136] transforms this text into a revelation of character perception (an example of extra-diegetic typography). The narrational behavior of this skeuomorphic text integrates crediting and typography with the visual space, forcing the acknowledgment that when text is (super)imposed as an independent element it ruptures the diegesis. The historically 'remote' example of *The Cabinet of Dr. Caligari* thus becomes paradigmatic for a realist integration of type and image, neither irrelevant nor ignorable in the lineage of on-screen typography. This same approach to integrating typography appears throughout *The Life of Brian* title sequence, not only as integrations of text-animation, but in the ways that letters imitate both neon tubes and ancient building blocks at the start of the title sequence, and are embedded within/as the graphics throughout. Skeuomorphic imitation appears in the studio logos rendered as cobblestones in the opening shots of *Sherlock Holmes*, allowing the elimination of any superimpositions by replacing them with the immanence of type within the diegetic space; ironically, these plastic transformations of the image affirm its constructed nature even as they present it as a continuous, autonomous 'space.' The main title card in *Sucker Punch* integrates the type into the visual space on-screen even more dynamically as streams of water that momentarily form the title card as the music crescendos. In each case, the transfer between *being-external* (type) and *being-internal* (graphic) to the visual space links these later photorealistic animations to the early integration of type in *The Cabinet of Doctor Caligari*: what distinguishes them is their technology of production and naturalistic affect, rather than their narrational interiority or diegetic presence within the images/scenes shown on-screen.

The superficial inevitability of 'realism' for motion graphics originates with the problematics of combining text and image. The opposition of reading and seeing—*you read the words first*—challenges the integral and coherent nature of the world-on-screen in ways that are resolved through a prohibition on text as a rupture of that illusion. This conception of language as an imposed externality finds superficial support in the obvious fact of it requiring a specialized, technical production separate from the live action photography of the background imagery. Motion graphics and the title sequence connect digital cinema to the basis of motion pictures in photographic technology. For realist ideology, the creation of the diegesis is fragile, easily challenged and disrupted—a peculiar belief given how dominant and autonomous it is, a morphology and structure of interpretation informing so much of how audiences understand motion pictures. The historical instability of "pure" media only poses definitional and conceptual problems for those works primarily considered within that Modernist paradigm: the marginalized and neglected hybrid forms—readily apparent in the convergent role of animation, optical printing, avant-garde film, and graphic design in commercial motion graphics—offer a tangential conception of cinema, one that is neither tied to the purist conception of *cinema=narrative*, nor to a restrictive conception of technical determinism and ontological belief. The complex interpretations that shift between *being-image* and *being-type*—not merely the familiar dynamic of visuality::legibility, such as skeuomorphic typography that changes its 'identity' during its time on-screen—mediates against this displacement, offering the *crediting function* an integral role in the semiosis, rather than its more standard conception in commercial realism as an oppositional aspect of interpretation that disrupts the world-on-screen. The 'reading-image' displaces *fabula* and narration with the procedural engagement of lexicality, accommodating typo/graphics within the familiar range of naturalism::stylization, thus announcing the dominant, realist ideology in commercial cinema and motion graphics, a socio-political effect unfamiliar in the static compositions of graphic design.

Notes

1 Bordwell, D. "Intensified Continuity: Visual Style in Contemporary American Film" *Film Quarterly* vol. 55, no. 3. (Spring 2002) pp. 16–28.
2 Hagener, M., Hediger V. and Strohmaier, A. *The State of Post-Cinema* (London: Palgrave, 2016) pp. 3–7.
3 McMurtrie, D. "The Philosophy of Modernism in Typography" *Texts on Type* ed. Steven Heller and Phillip Meggs (New York: Allworth Press, 2001) p. 147.
4 Jakobson, R. *Selected Writings III: Poetry of Grammar and Grammar of Poetry* (New York: Mouton Publishers, 1981) pp. 22–26.
5 Foucault, M. *This is not a Pipe* (Berkeley: University of California Press, 1983), p. 58.
6 Deleuze, G. *Cinema 1: The Movement-Image* (Minneapolis: The University of Minnesota Press, 1989) np.
7 Betancourt, M. *Title Sequences as Paratexts: Narrative Anticipation and Recapitulation* (New York: Routledge Focus, 2018).
8 Călinescu, M. *The Five Faces of Modernity* (Durham: Duke University Press: 1987).
9 Saussure, F. *Course in General Linguistics* (New York: 1966).
10 Rorty, R. "The Pragmatist's Progress" *Interpretation and Overinterpretation* ed. Stefan Collini (New York: Cambridge University Press, 1996) pp. 89–108.
11 Barnett, D. *Movement as Meaning in Experimental Film* (New York: Rodopi, 2008) pp. 16–18.
12 Barnett, D. *Movement as Meaning in Experimental Film* (New York: Rodopi, 2008) pp. 28–29.
13 Altman, R. "General Introduction: Cinema as Event" *Sound Theory, Sound Practice* (New York: Routledge, 1992) pp. 2–4.
14 Derrida, J. *Of Grammatology* trans. Gayatri Chakravorty Spivak (Baltimore: The Johns Hopkins University Press, 1977).
15 Eco, U. *Kant and the Platypus* (New York: Harvest Books, 2000) pp. 125–126.
16 Ziehen, T. *Lehrbuch der Logik auf positivistischer Grundlage mit Berücksichtigung der Geschichte der Logik* (Bonn: A. Marcus & E. Webere Verlag, 1920).
17 Shaviro, S. *Post Cinematic Affect* (Washington: Zero Books, 2010) pp. 132–133.
18 Berry, D. and Dieter, M. "Thinking Postdigital Aesthetics: Art, Computation, Design" *The State of Post-Cinema* ed. Berry, D. and Dieter, M. (New York: Palgrave Macmillan, 2015) pp. 2–3.
19 Pangrazio, L. and Bishop, C. "Art as Digital Counterpractice" *CTheory* (May 24, 2017) ctheory.net/ctheory_wp/art-as-digital-counterpractice/.

20 Berry, D. and Dieter, M. "Thinking Postdigital Aesthetics: Art, Computation, Design" *The State of Post-Cinema* ed. Berry, D. and Dieter, M. (New York: Palgrave Macmillan, 2015) pp. 2–3.
21 Hagener, M., Hediger V. and Strohmaier, A. *The State of Post-Cinema* (London: Palgrave, 2016) p. 4.
22 Gaudreault, A. and Marion, P. *Kinematic Turn: Film in the Digital Era and Its Ten Problems* trans. Timothy Barnard (Montreal: Caboose Books, 2012) p. 40.
23 McFarlen, Z. "The Narrative Implications of Kinetic Typography in *Scott Pilgrim vs. the World*" *Motion Design Education Summit: 2015 Conference Proceedings* (New York: Focal Press, 2016) pp. 171–182.
24 Eco, U. *The Limits of Interpretation* (Bloomington: Indiana University Press, 1994) p. 104.
25 Foucault, M. *The Birth of the Clinic* (New York: Vintage, 1975) p. xiii.
26 Penner, N. "Rethinking the Diegetic/Nondiegetic Distinction in the Film Musical" *Music and the Moving Image* vol. 10, no. 3. (Fall 2017) pp. 3–6.

Index